Year: _____

Model #: _____

Location:_____

_____

According to OSHA regulations, forklift inspections should be conducted on a daily basis at the start of the operator's shift. It is the operator's responsibility to fully inspect the forklift before it is placed into service and report any abnormalities to their supervisor. Operations that run multiple shifts are required to perform a pre-use inspection at the beginning of every shift.

A proper pre-use inspection consists of two parts:

- Visual Inspection
- Operational Inspection

Let's take a closer look.

Visual Inspection

You may be asking yourself, what should I be checking when conducting a walk around inspection? Here's a list of the things you should be checking:

- **Tires**: Ensure the forklift's tires are in good condition. Check for slashes, cuts and air pressure in pneumatic tires.
- **Hoses, Belts & Chains**: Inspect these for excessive wear. Things to look out for are cracks, pinholes or leaks. SAFETY TIP: NEVER place your fingers inside the mast.
- **Fluid Levels**: Check hydraulic fluid levels and ensure there are no leaks.
- **Engine / Power Source**: Check engine in IC forklifts and check the power source in electric forklifts.
- **Forks, Backrest, Mast, & Overhead Guard**: Check each piece for cracks, dents, broken welds or any other irregularities.
- **Data Plate & Labels**: Ensure both the data plate and any warning labels are legible.

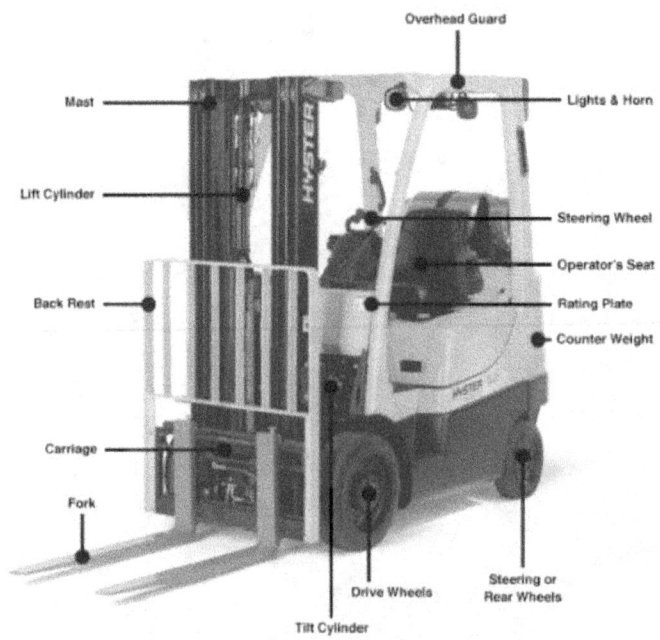

Operational Inspection

Now that you have completed the walk around inspection; let's move onto the seated portion. Climb into your forklift using three points of contact. While seated check the following:

- **Seat Belt**: Check the seat belt is in good condition and fasten it securely.
- **Gauges, Warning Lights, & Fuel Levels**: Turn on your forklift and check the gauges, warning light and battery/fuel levels. You should ALWAYS be seated when you turn on a forklift. Do not attempt to start the engine while standing outside the forklift.
- **Safety Equipment**: Check any safety equipment such as a safety lights to ensure they're working properly.
- **Controls**: Use the controls to lift/lower the forks and to tilt the mast and check they're operating smoothly.
- **Horn**: Honk to test your horn is working. Remember to always honk at intersections.
- **Brakes**: Allow the forklift to move forward and then step on the brake to ensure it's working smoothly and reliably.
- **Steering**: Check the steering. Note that hard steering may reduce your control.
- Parking **Brake**: Set and test the parking brake. Don't forget to put the controls in neutral. At this time, get out of the forklift and check for leaks. Leaks can signal a hydraulic issue. Any fluid left on the floor could also result as a slipping hazard.
- Exhaus**t System**: Check to see if there are any sparks or flames coming from the exhaust and listen for any unusual sounds.

-

Removal from service

While driving the forklift, if the operator faces any of the following conditions, they must stop, park the vehicle and get assistance –

1. **Mechanical breakdown** – If the forklift is not in safe condition or found with defects, it should be removed from service.
2. **Fire** – If there are hazardous sparks or flames from the exhaust system, the forklift should be discontinued from service till it is repaired.
3. **Overheating** – When the temperature of any part of the forklift increases beyond normal, the vehicle should be removed from service.
4. **Leakage** – No forklift shall be operated with a leak in the fuel system.

- Look out for any leaks, cracks, or visible defects in hydraulic hoses or tension in mast chains. – Checking for wet spots around hoses is how to identify hydraulic leaks, look visually around the hose connectors for cracks and bulges. Check along loop points for cracks, bulges, and frayed spots.

- Check fork condition including the top clip retaining pin and heel. – Forks should be able to be moved. Also inspect the tips of the forks, for curling or cracking.

- Check the load backrest extension and see if finger guards are attached. – Load backrest should be free from dents, deflections, or damage.

- Propane connectors for frayed tube or leaking connections. – propane connectors can become damaged over time, so visually inspect the cables and connectors for fraying on the cable and cracks or leaks on the connectors.

- Check if the **accelerator** or direction control pedal is working smoothly. – Inspect these as an operation test, by slowly moving the equipment.

- Tilt control: forward and back should be checked for smooth functioning. – Tilt the mast forward and back, quickly to verify operation is smooth and responsive.

Week Ending: _____

The equipment operator must make this check daily at the start of the shift.

Check the appropriate box if the item is OK. If there is a problem with the item, leave the space blank and fill out the COMMENTS section below.

Visual Checks	Sun	Mon	Tues	Wed	Thur	Fri	Sat
EXCESS DIRT AND DEBRIS							
DAMAGE (Bent, dented or broken parts, paint transfer)							
LEAKS (Drive unit, brakes, hydraulics)							
TIRES & WHEELS (Drive wheels, load wheels, casters)							
FORKS (In place, properly secured, locking pins)							
CHAINS, CABLES, HOSES (In place)							
GUAGES (Operating)							
PROPANE BOTLE (relief valve, safety strap, fuel level, listen for leaks)							
ENGINE COMPARTMENT (oil, fan belt, battery, etc…)							
GUARDS (Overhead, load backrest, mast, etc.)							
SAFETY DEVICES (<u>Lights</u>, labels, seatbelt, harness, tether)							
MAST ASSEMBLY (no broken welds, no dents)							
Operational Checks			REPORT ALL UNSAFE CONDITIONS				
HORN (Sounds)							
STEERING (No binding, no excessive play)							
TRAVEL CONTROLS (All speed ranges, forward/reverse, etc.)							
HYDRAULIC CONTROLS (Raise & lover, tilt forward & back)							
BRAKES (Stop truck within required distance)							
PARKING BRAKE (Seat, hand, foot)							
POWER DISCONNECT (Cuts off all electric power)							
ATTACHMENTS (Function properly)							
EQUIPMENT WAS NOT USED ON THIS PARTICULAR DAY.							
OPERATOR'S INITIALS (PLEASE PRINT CLEARLY)							

Supervisor's Initials upon review:_____

COMMENTS: (Items needing repair or adjustment)

Date:	Issue:
Resolved Date:	**Resolved By:**
COMMENTS	

CAUTION: If the equipment is found to be in need of repair or in any way unsafe, or contributes to an unsafe condition, the matter shall be reported immediately to the designated authority and the equipment shall not be operated until it has been restored to safe condition. Do not make repairs or adjustments unless specifically authorized to do so.

- Inspect tire condition:
    - Pneumatic(air filled) wheels should have pressure and now have cracks through the rubber.
    - Solid wheels should not have large cracks or gouges in them.

- Check for grease and debris in the operator compartment – this can contribute to slipping off the equipment, and cause a serious injury.

- Hood & panel latches – Does the hood and any removable side panels secure in place to no avoid opening or falling off.

- Steering should function smoothly – while testing this, ensure the steering wheel solidly reacts to movements. This should always be monitored during operation.

- Check the functioning of horn and lights – this test is as simple as ensuring the lights aren't burnt out, and the horn operates.

- Back-up alarm (if equipped) should be checked – A backup alarm is a helpful piece of safety equipment. If equipped it must be operational, and not covered in any sound dampening material.

Week Ending: _____							
The equipment operator must make this check daily at the start of the shift.							
Check the appropriate box if the item is OK. If there is a problem with the item, leave the space blank and fill out the COMMENTS section below.							
Visual Checks	Sun	Mon	Tues	Wed	Thur	Fri	Sat
EXCESS DIRT AND DEBRIS							
DAMAGE (Bent, dented or broken parts, paint transfer)							
LEAKS (Drive unit, brakes, hydraulics)							
TIRES & WHEELS (Drive wheels, load wheels, casters)							
FORKS (In place, properly secured, locking pins)							
CHAINS, CABLES, HOSES (In place)							
GUAGES (Operating)							
PROPANE BOTLE (relief valve, safety strap, fuel level, listen for leaks)							
ENGINE COMPARTMENT (oil, fan belt, battery, etc...)							
GUARDS (Overhead, load backrest, mast, etc.)							
SAFETY DEVICES (<u>Lights</u>, labels, seatbelt, harness, tether)							
MAST ASSEMBLY (no broken welds, no dents)							
Operational Checks	**REPORT ALL UNSAFE CONDITIONS**						
HORN (Sounds)							
STEERING (No binding, no excessive play)							
TRAVEL CONTROLS (All speed ranges, forward/reverse, etc.)							
HYDRAULIC CONTROLS (Raise & lover, tilt forward & back)							
BRAKES (Stop truck within required distance)							
PARKING BRAKE (Seat, hand, foot)							
POWER DISCONNECT (Cuts off all electric power)							
ATTACHMENTS (Function properly)							
EQUIPMENT WAS NOT USED ON THIS PARTICULAR DAY.							
OPERATOR'S INITIALS (PLEASE PRINT CLEARLY)							
Supervisor's Initials upon review:_____							

COMMENTS: (Items needing repair or adjustment)

Date:	Issue:
Resolved Date:	**Resolved By:**
COMMENTS	

CAUTION: If the equipment is found to be in need of repair or in any way unsafe, or contributes to an unsafe condition, the matter shall be reported immediately to the designated authority and the equipment shall not be operated until it has been restored to safe condition. Do not make repairs or adjustments unless specifically authorized to do so.

- Verify that all safety devices like the seat belt is in proper working condition – The seatbelt should be checked to ensure it locks on quick stops, and that it securely closes.

- Propane bottle restraints – The propane bottle should be secured in place with restraints, which must be locked in place.

- Propane level and connections – Check the level of the propane and the connection points, to ensure you have plenty of fuel for the safe operation and that it isn't leaking.

- Drive control - forward and reverse should be checked for smooth functioning.

- Hoist and lowering control should function smoothly – Check this by raising and lowering the mast, also at this point check the chain, to make sure it has adequate tension.

- Gauges: Functioning of Amp meter, engine oil pressure, Hour Meter, fuel level, temperature, and instrument monitors.

Week Ending: _____

The equipment operator must make this check daily at the start of the shift.

Check the appropriate box if the item is OK. If there is a problem with the item, leave the space blank and fill out the COMMENTS section below.

Visual Checks	Sun	Mon	Tues	Wed	Thur	Fri	Sat
EXCESS DIRT AND DEBRIS							
DAMAGE (Bent, dented or broken parts, paint transfer)							
LEAKS (Drive unit, brakes, hydraulics)							
TIRES & WHEELS (Drive wheels, load wheels, casters)							
FORKS (In place, properly secured, locking pins)							
CHAINS, CABLES, HOSES (In place)							
GUAGES (Operating)							
PROPANE BOTLE (relief valve, safety strap, fuel level, listen for leaks)							
ENGINE COMPARTMENT (oil, fan belt, battery, etc...)							
GUARDS (Overhead, load backrest, mast, etc.)							
SAFETY DEVICES (<u>Lights</u>, labels, seatbelt, harness, tether)							
MAST ASSEMBLY (no broken welds, no dents)							
Operational Checks	REPORT ALL UNSAFE CONDITIONS						
HORN (Sounds)							
STEERING (No binding, no excessive play)							
TRAVEL CONTROLS (All speed ranges, forward/reverse, etc.)							
HYDRAULIC CONTROLS (Raise & lover, tilt forward & back)							
BRAKES (Stop truck within required distance)							
PARKING BRAKE (Seat, hand, foot)							
POWER DISCONNECT (Cuts off all electric power)							
ATTACHMENTS (Function properly)							
EQUIPMENT WAS NOT USED ON THIS PARTICULAR DAY.							
OPERATOR'S INITIALS (PLEASE PRINT CLEARLY)							
Supervisor's Initials upon review:_____							

COMMENTS: (Items needing repair or adjustment)

Date:	Issue:
Resolved Date:	**Resolved By:**
COMMENTS	

CAUTION: If the equipment is found to be in need of repair or in any way unsafe, or contributes to an unsafe condition, the matter shall be reported immediately to the designated authority and the equipment shall not be operated until it has been restored to safe condition. Do not make repairs or adjustments unless specifically authorized to do so.

- Inspect tire condition:
  - Pneumatic(air filled) wheels should have pressure and now have cracks through the rubber.
  - Solid wheels should not have large cracks or gouges in them.

- Check for grease and debris in the operator compartment – this can contribute to slipping off the equipment, and cause a serious injury.

- Hood & panel latches – Does the hood and any removable side panels secure in place to no avoid opening or falling off.

- Steering should function smoothly – while testing this, ensure the steering wheel solidly reacts to movements. This should always be monitored during operation.

- Check the functioning of horn and lights – this test is as simple as ensuring the lights aren't burnt out, and the horn operates.

- Back-up alarm (if equipped) should be checked – A backup alarm is a helpful piece of safety equipment. If equipped it must be operational, and not covered in any sound dampening material.

Week Ending: _____

The equipment operator must make this check daily at the start of the shift.

Check the appropriate box if the item is OK. If there is a problem with the item, leave the space blank and fill out the COMMENTS section below.

Visual Checks	Sun	Mon	Tues	Wed	Thur	Fri	Sat
EXCESS DIRT AND DEBRIS							
DAMAGE (Bent, dented or broken parts, paint transfer)							
LEAKS (Drive unit, brakes, hydraulics)							
TIRES & WHEELS (Drive wheels, load wheels, casters)							
FORKS (In place, properly secured, locking pins)							
CHAINS, CABLES, HOSES (In place)							
GUAGES (Operating)							
PROPANE BOTLE (relief valve, safety strap, fuel level, listen for leaks)							
ENGINE COMPARTMENT (oil, fan belt, battery, etc...)							
GUARDS (Overhead, load backrest, mast, etc.)							
SAFETY DEVICES (<u>Lights</u>, labels, seatbelt, harness, tether)							
MAST ASSEMBLY (no broken welds, no dents)							
Operational Checks	**REPORT ALL UNSAFE CONDITIONS**						
HORN (Sounds)							
STEERING (No binding, no excessive play)							
TRAVEL CONTROLS (All speed ranges, forward/reverse, etc.)							
HYDRAULIC CONTROLS (Raise & lover, tilt forward & back)							
BRAKES (Stop truck within required distance)							
PARKING BRAKE (Seat, hand, foot)							
POWER DISCONNECT (Cuts off all electric power)							
ATTACHMENTS (Function properly)							
EQUIPMENT WAS NOT USED ON THIS PARTICULAR DAY.							
OPERATOR'S INITIALS (PLEASE PRINT CLEARLY)							
Supervisor's Initials upon review:_____							

COMMENTS: (Items needing repair or adjustment)

Date:	Issue:
Resolved Date:	**Resolved By:**
COMMENTS	

CAUTION: If the equipment is found to be in need of repair or in any way unsafe, or contributes to an unsafe condition, the matter shall be reported immediately to the designated authority and the equipment shall not be operated until it has been restored to safe condition. Do not make repairs or adjustments unless specifically authorized to do so.

- Look out for any leaks, cracks, or visible defects in hydraulic hoses or tension in mast chains. – Checking for wet spots around hoses is how to identify hydraulic leaks, look visually around the hose connectors for cracks and bulges. Check along loop points for cracks, bulges, and frayed spots.

- Check fork condition including the top clip retaining pin and heel. – Forks should be able to be moved. Also inspect the tips of the forks, for curling or cracking.

- Check the load backrest extension and see if finger guards are attached. – Load backrest should be free from dents, deflections, or damage.

- Propane connectors for frayed tube or leaking connections. – propane connectors can become damaged over time, so visually inspect the cables and connectors for fraying on the cable and cracks or leaks on the connectors.

- Check if the **accelerator** or direction control pedal is working smoothly. – Inspect these as an operation test, by slowly moving the equipment.

- Tilt control: forward and back should be checked for smooth functioning. – Tilt the mast forward and back, quickly to verify operation is smooth and responsive.

Week Ending: _____

The equipment operator must make this check daily at the start of the shift.

Check the appropriate box if the item is OK. If there is a problem with the item, leave the space blank and fill out the COMMENTS section below.

Visual Checks	Sun	Mon	Tues	Wed	Thur	Fri	Sat
EXCESS DIRT AND DEBRIS							
DAMAGE (Bent, dented or broken parts, paint transfer)							
LEAKS (Drive unit, brakes, hydraulics)							
TIRES & WHEELS (Drive wheels, load wheels, casters)							
FORKS (In place, properly secured, locking pins)							
CHAINS, CABLES, HOSES (In place)							
GUAGES (Operating)							
PROPANE BOTLE (relief valve, safety strap, fuel level, listen for leaks)							
ENGINE COMPARTMENT (oil, fan belt, battery, etc...)							
GUARDS (Overhead, load backrest, mast, etc.)							
SAFETY DEVICES (<u>Lights</u>, labels, seatbelt, harness, tether)							
MAST ASSEMBLY (no broken welds, no dents)							
Operational Checks	**REPORT ALL UNSAFE CONDITIONS**						
HORN (Sounds)							
STEERING (No binding, no excessive play)							
TRAVEL CONTROLS (All speed ranges, forward/reverse, etc.)							
HYDRAULIC CONTROLS (Raise & lover, tilt forward & back)							
BRAKES (Stop truck within required distance)							
PARKING BRAKE (Seat, hand, foot)							
POWER DISCONNECT (Cuts off all electric power)							
ATTACHMENTS (Function properly)							
EQUIPMENT WAS NOT USED ON THIS PARTICULAR DAY.							
OPERATOR'S INITIALS (PLEASE PRINT CLEARLY)							
Supervisor's Initials upon review:_____							

COMMENTS: (Items needing repair or adjustment)

Date:	Issue:
Resolved Date:	**Resolved By:**
COMMENTS	

CAUTION: If the equipment is found to be in need of repair or in any way unsafe, or contributes to an unsafe condition, the matter shall be reported immediately to the designated authority and the equipment shall not be operated until it has been restored to safe condition. Do not make repairs or adjustments unless specifically authorized to do so.

- Inspect tire condition:
  - Pneumatic(air filled) wheels should have pressure and now have cracks through the rubber.
  - Solid wheels should not have large cracks or gouges in them.

- Check for grease and debris in the operator compartment – this can contribute to slipping off the equipment, and cause a serious injury.

- Hood & panel latches – Does the hood and any removable side panels secure in place to no avoid opening or falling off.

- Steering should function smoothly – while testing this, ensure the steering wheel solidly reacts to movements. This should always be monitored during operation.

- Check the functioning of horn and lights – this test is as simple as ensuring the lights aren't burnt out, and the horn operates.

- Back-up alarm (if equipped) should be checked – A backup alarm is a helpful piece of safety equipment. If equipped it must be operational, and not covered in any sound dampening material.

Week Ending: _____							
The equipment operator must make this check daily at the start of the shift.							
Check the appropriate box if the item is OK. If there is a problem with the item, leave the space blank and fill out the COMMENTS section below.							

Visual Checks	Sun	Mon	Tues	Wed	Thur	Fri	Sat
EXCESS DIRT AND DEBRIS							
DAMAGE (Bent, dented or broken parts, paint transfer)							
LEAKS (Drive unit, brakes, hydraulics)							
TIRES & WHEELS (Drive wheels, load wheels, casters)							
FORKS (In place, properly secured, locking pins)							
CHAINS, CABLES, HOSES (In place)							
GUAGES (Operating)							
PROPANE BOTLE (relief valve, safety strap, fuel level, listen for leaks)							
ENGINE COMPARTMENT (oil, fan belt, battery, etc...)							
GUARDS (Overhead, load backrest, mast, etc.)							
SAFETY DEVICES (Lights, labels, seatbelt, harness, tether)							
MAST ASSEMBLY (no broken welds, no dents)							
Operational Checks	**REPORT ALL UNSAFE CONDITIONS**						
HORN (Sounds)							
STEERING (No binding, no excessive play)							
TRAVEL CONTROLS (All speed ranges, forward/reverse, etc.)							
HYDRAULIC CONTROLS (Raise & lover, tilt forward & back)							
BRAKES (Stop truck within required distance)							
PARKING BRAKE (Seat, hand, foot)							
POWER DISCONNECT (Cuts off all electric power)							
ATTACHMENTS (Function properly)							
EQUIPMENT WAS NOT USED ON THIS PARTICULAR DAY.							
OPERATOR'S INITIALS (PLEASE PRINT CLEARLY)							
Supervisor's Initials upon review:_____							

COMMENTS: (Items needing repair or adjustment)

Date:	Issue:
Resolved Date:	Resolved By:
COMMENTS	

CAUTION: If the equipment is found to be in need of repair or in any way unsafe, or contributes to an unsafe condition, the matter shall be reported immediately to the designated authority and the equipment shall not be operated until it has been restored to safe condition. Do not make repairs or adjustments unless specifically authorized to do so.

- Verify that all safety devices like the seat belt is in proper working condition – The seatbelt should be checked to ensure it locks on quick stops, and that it securely closes.

- Propane bottle restraints – The propane bottle should be secured in place with restraints, which must be locked in place.

- Propane level and connections – Check the level of the propane and the connection points, to ensure you have plenty of fuel for the safe operation and that it isn't leaking.

- Drive control - forward and reverse should be checked for smooth functioning.

- Hoist and lowering control should function smoothly – Check this by raising and lowering the mast, also at this point check the chain, to make sure it has adequate tension.

- Gauges: Functioning of Amp meter, engine oil pressure, Hour Meter, fuel level, temperature, and instrument monitors.

Week Ending: _____

The equipment operator must make this check daily at the start of the shift.

Check the appropriate box if the item is OK. If there is a problem with the item, leave the space blank and fill out the COMMENTS section below.

Visual Checks	Sun	Mon	Tues	Wed	Thur	Fri	Sat
EXCESS DIRT AND DEBRIS							
DAMAGE (Bent, dented or broken parts, paint transfer)							
LEAKS (Drive unit, brakes, hydraulics)							
TIRES & WHEELS (Drive wheels, load wheels, casters)							
FORKS (In place, properly secured, locking pins)							
CHAINS, CABLES, HOSES (In place)							
GUAGES (Operating)							
PROPANE BOTLE (relief valve, safety strap, fuel level, listen for leaks)							
ENGINE COMPARTMENT (oil, fan belt, battery, etc…)							
GUARDS (Overhead, load backrest, mast, etc.)							
SAFETY DEVICES (<u>Lights</u>, labels, seatbelt, harness, tether)							
MAST ASSEMBLY (no broken welds, no dents)							
Operational Checks		**REPORT ALL UNSAFE CONDITIONS**					
HORN (Sounds)							
STEERING (No binding, no excessive play)							
TRAVEL CONTROLS (All speed ranges, forward/reverse, etc.)							
HYDRAULIC CONTROLS (Raise & lover, tilt forward & back)							
BRAKES (Stop truck within required distance)							
PARKING BRAKE (Seat, hand, foot)							
POWER DISCONNECT (Cuts off all electric power)							
ATTACHMENTS (Function properly)							
EQUIPMENT WAS NOT USED ON THIS PARTICULAR DAY.							
OPERATOR'S INITIALS (PLEASE PRINT CLEARLY)							

Supervisor's Initials upon review:_____

COMMENTS: (Items needing repair or adjustment)

Date:	Issue:
Resolved Date:	**Resolved By:**
COMMENTS	

CAUTION: If the equipment is found to be in need of repair or in any way unsafe, or contributes to an unsafe condition, the matter shall be reported immediately to the designated authority and the equipment shall not be operated until it has been restored to safe condition. Do not make repairs or adjustments unless specifically authorized to do so.

- Inspect tire condition:
    - Pneumatic(air filled) wheels should have pressure and now have cracks through the rubber.
    - Solid wheels should not have large cracks or gouges in them.

- Check for grease and debris in the operator compartment – this can contribute to slipping off the equipment, and cause a serious injury.

- Hood & panel latches – Does the hood and any removable side panels secure in place to no avoid opening or falling off.

- Steering should function smoothly – while testing this, ensure the steering wheel solidly reacts to movements. This should always be monitored during operation.

- Check the functioning of horn and lights – this test is as simple as ensuring the lights aren't burnt out, and the horn operates.

- Back-up alarm (if equipped) should be checked – A backup alarm is a helpful piece of safety equipment. If equipped it must be operational, and not covered in any sound dampening material.

Week Ending: _____

The equipment operator must make this check daily at the start of the shift.

Check the appropriate box if the item is OK. If there is a problem with the item, leave the space blank and fill out the COMMENTS section below.

Visual Checks	Sun	Mon	Tues	Wed	Thur	Fri	Sat
EXCESS DIRT AND DEBRIS							
DAMAGE (Bent, dented or broken parts, paint transfer)							
LEAKS (Drive unit, brakes, hydraulics)							
TIRES & WHEELS (Drive wheels, load wheels, casters)							
FORKS (In place, properly secured, locking pins)							
CHAINS, CABLES, HOSES (In place)							
GUAGES (Operating)							
PROPANE BOTLE (relief valve, safety strap, fuel level, listen for leaks)							
ENGINE COMPARTMENT (oil, fan belt, battery, etc...)							
GUARDS (Overhead, load backrest, mast, etc.)							
SAFETY DEVICES (<u>Lights</u>, labels, seatbelt, harness, tether)							
MAST ASSEMBLY (no broken welds, no dents)							
Operational Checks	**REPORT ALL UNSAFE CONDITIONS**						
HORN (Sounds)							
STEERING (No binding, no excessive play)							
TRAVEL CONTROLS (All speed ranges, forward/reverse, etc.)							
HYDRAULIC CONTROLS (Raise & lover, tilt forward & back)							
BRAKES (Stop truck within required distance)							
PARKING BRAKE (Seat, hand, foot)							
POWER DISCONNECT (Cuts off all electric power)							
ATTACHMENTS (Function properly)							
EQUIPMENT WAS NOT USED ON THIS PARTICULAR DAY.							
OPERATOR'S INITIALS (PLEASE PRINT CLEARLY)							
Supervisor's Initials upon review:_____							

COMMENTS: (Items needing repair or adjustment)

Date:	Issue:
Resolved Date:	Resolved By:
COMMENTS	

CAUTION: If the equipment is found to be in need of repair or in any way unsafe, or contributes to an unsafe condition, the matter shall be reported immediately to the designated authority and the equipment shall not be operated until it has been restored to safe condition. Do not make repairs or adjustments unless specifically authorized to do so.

- Look out for any leaks, cracks, or visible defects in hydraulic hoses or tension in mast chains. – Checking for wet spots around hoses is how to identify hydraulic leaks, look visually around the hose connectors for cracks and bulges. Check along loop points for cracks, bulges, and frayed spots.

- Check fork condition including the top clip retaining pin and heel. – Forks should be able to be moved. Also inspect the tips of the forks, for curling or cracking.

- Check the load backrest extension and see if finger guards are attached. – Load backrest should be free from dents, deflections, or damage.

- Propane connectors for frayed tube or leaking connections. – propane connectors can become damaged over time, so visually inspect the cables and connectors for fraying on the cable and cracks or leaks on the connectors.

- Check if the **accelerator** or direction control pedal is working smoothly. – Inspect these as an operation test, by slowly moving the equipment.

- Tilt control: forward and back should be checked for smooth functioning. – Tilt the mast forward and back, quickly to verify operation is smooth and responsive.

Week Ending: _____

The equipment operator must make this check daily at the start of the shift.

Check the appropriate box if the item is OK. If there is a problem with the item, leave the space blank and fill out the COMMENTS section below.

Visual Checks	Sun	Mon	Tues	Wed	Thur	Fri	Sat
EXCESS DIRT AND DEBRIS							
DAMAGE (Bent, dented or broken parts, paint transfer)							
LEAKS (Drive unit, brakes, hydraulics)							
TIRES & WHEELS (Drive wheels, load wheels, casters)							
FORKS (In place, properly secured, locking pins)							
CHAINS, CABLES, HOSES (In place)							
GUAGES (Operating)							
PROPANE BOTLE (relief valve, safety strap, fuel level, listen for leaks)							
ENGINE COMPARTMENT (oil, fan belt, battery, etc...)							
GUARDS (Overhead, load backrest, mast, etc.)							
SAFETY DEVICES (<u>Lights</u>, labels, seatbelt, harness, tether)							
MAST ASSEMBLY (no broken welds, no dents)							
Operational Checks	REPORT ALL UNSAFE CONDITIONS						
HORN (Sounds)							
STEERING (No binding, no excessive play)							
TRAVEL CONTROLS (All speed ranges, forward/reverse, etc.)							
HYDRAULIC CONTROLS (Raise & lover, tilt forward & back)							
BRAKES (Stop truck within required distance)							
PARKING BRAKE (Seat, hand, foot)							
POWER DISCONNECT (Cuts off all electric power)							
ATTACHMENTS (Function properly)							
EQUIPMENT WAS NOT USED ON THIS PARTICULAR DAY.							
OPERATOR'S INITIALS (PLEASE PRINT CLEARLY)							
Supervisor's Initials upon review:_____							

COMMENTS: (Items needing repair or adjustment)

Date:	Issue:
Resolved Date:	**Resolved By:**
COMMENTS	

CAUTION: If the equipment is found to be in need of repair or in any way unsafe, or contributes to an unsafe condition, the matter shall be reported immediately to the designated authority and the equipment shall not be operated until it has been restored to safe condition. Do not make repairs or adjustments unless specifically authorized to do so.

- Inspect tire condition:
    - Pneumatic(air filled) wheels should have pressure and now have cracks through the rubber.
    - Solid wheels should not have large cracks or gouges in them.

- Check for grease and debris in the operator compartment – this can contribute to slipping off the equipment, and cause a serious injury.

- Hood & panel latches – Does the hood and any removable side panels secure in place to no avoid opening or falling off.

- Steering should function smoothly – while testing this, ensure the steering wheel solidly reacts to movements. This should always be monitored during operation.

- Check the functioning of horn and lights – this test is as simple as ensuring the lights aren't burnt out, and the horn operates.

- Back-up alarm (if equipped) should be checked – A backup alarm is a helpful piece of safety equipment. If equipped it must be operational, and not covered in any sound dampening material.

Week Ending: _____

The equipment operator must make this check daily at the start of the shift.

Check the appropriate box if the item is OK. If there is a problem with the item, leave the space blank and fill out the COMMENTS section below.

Visual Checks	Sun	Mon	Tues	Wed	Thur	Fri	Sat
EXCESS DIRT AND DEBRIS							
DAMAGE (Bent, dented or broken parts, paint transfer)							
LEAKS (Drive unit, brakes, hydraulics)							
TIRES & WHEELS (Drive wheels, load wheels, casters)							
FORKS (In place, properly secured, locking pins)							
CHAINS, CABLES, HOSES (In place)							
GUAGES (Operating)							
PROPANE BOTLE (relief valve, safety strap, fuel level, listen for leaks)							
ENGINE COMPARTMENT (oil, fan belt, battery, etc…)							
GUARDS (Overhead, load backrest, mast, etc.)							
SAFETY DEVICES (<u>Lights</u>, labels, seatbelt, harness, tether)							
MAST ASSEMBLY (no broken welds, no dents)							
Operational Checks	**REPORT ALL UNSAFE CONDITIONS**						
HORN (Sounds)							
STEERING (No binding, no excessive play)							
TRAVEL CONTROLS (All speed ranges, forward/reverse, etc.)							
HYDRAULIC CONTROLS (Raise & lover, tilt forward & back)							
BRAKES (Stop truck within required distance)							
PARKING BRAKE (Seat, hand, foot)							
POWER DISCONNECT (Cuts off all electric power)							
ATTACHMENTS (Function properly)							
EQUIPMENT WAS NOT USED ON THIS PARTICULAR DAY.							
OPERATOR'S INITIALS (PLEASE PRINT CLEARLY)							

Supervisor's Initials upon review:_____

COMMENTS: (Items needing repair or adjustment)

Date:	Issue:
Resolved Date:	**Resolved By:**
COMMENTS	

CAUTION: If the equipment is found to be in need of repair or in any way unsafe, or contributes to an unsafe condition, the matter shall be reported immediately to the designated authority and the equipment shall not be operated until it has been restored to safe condition. Do not make repairs or adjustments unless specifically authorized to do so.

- Verify that all safety devices like the seat belt is in proper working condition – The seatbelt should be checked to ensure it locks on quick stops, and that it securely closes.

- Propane bottle restraints – The propane bottle should be secured in place with restraints, which must be locked in place.

- Propane level and connections – Check the level of the propane and the connection points, to ensure you have plenty of fuel for the safe operation and that it isn't leaking.

- Drive control - forward and reverse should be checked for smooth functioning.

- Hoist and lowering control should function smoothly – Check this by raising and lowering the mast, also at this point check the chain, to make sure it has adequate tension.

- Gauges: Functioning of Amp meter, engine oil pressure, Hour Meter, fuel level, temperature, and instrument monitors.

Week Ending: _____

The equipment operator must make this check daily at the start of the shift.

Check the appropriate box if the item is OK. If there is a problem with the item, leave the space blank and fill out the COMMENTS section below.

Visual Checks	Sun	Mon	Tues	Wed	Thur	Fri	Sat
EXCESS DIRT AND DEBRIS							
DAMAGE (Bent, dented or broken parts, paint transfer)							
LEAKS (Drive unit, brakes, hydraulics)							
TIRES & WHEELS (Drive wheels, load wheels, casters)							
FORKS (In place, properly secured, locking pins)							
CHAINS, CABLES, HOSES (In place)							
GUAGES (Operating)							
PROPANE BOTLE (relief valve, safety strap, fuel level, listen for leaks)							
ENGINE COMPARTMENT (oil, fan belt, battery, etc…)							
GUARDS (Overhead, load backrest, mast, etc.)							
SAFETY DEVICES (<u>Lights</u>, labels, seatbelt, harness, tether)							
MAST ASSEMBLY (no broken welds, no dents)							
Operational Checks	REPORT ALL UNSAFE CONDITIONS						
HORN (Sounds)							
STEERING (No binding, no excessive play)							
TRAVEL CONTROLS (All speed ranges, forward/reverse, etc.)							
HYDRAULIC CONTROLS (Raise & lover, tilt forward & back)							
BRAKES (Stop truck within required distance)							
PARKING BRAKE (Seat, hand, foot)							
POWER DISCONNECT (Cuts off all electric power)							
ATTACHMENTS (Function properly)							
EQUIPMENT WAS NOT USED ON THIS PARTICULAR DAY.							
OPERATOR'S INITIALS (PLEASE PRINT CLEARLY)							
Supervisor's Initials upon review:_____							

COMMENTS: (Items needing repair or adjustment)

Date:	Issue:
Resolved Date:	**Resolved By:**
COMMENTS	

CAUTION: If the equipment is found to be in need of repair or in any way unsafe, or contributes to an unsafe condition, the matter shall be reported immediately to the designated authority and the equipment shall not be operated until it has been restored to safe condition. Do not make repairs or adjustments unless specifically authorized to do so.

- Inspect tire condition:
  - Pneumatic(air filled) wheels should have pressure and now have cracks through the rubber.
  - Solid wheels should not have large cracks or gouges in them.

- Check for grease and debris in the operator compartment – this can contribute to slipping off the equipment, and cause a serious injury.

- Hood & panel latches – Does the hood and any removable side panels secure in place to no avoid opening or falling off.

- Steering should function smoothly – while testing this, ensure the steering wheel solidly reacts to movements. This should always be monitored during operation.

- Check the functioning of horn and lights – this test is as simple as ensuring the lights aren't burnt out, and the horn operates.

- Back-up alarm (if equipped) should be checked – A backup alarm is a helpful piece of safety equipment. If equipped it must be operational, and not covered in any sound dampening material.

Week Ending: _____

The equipment operator must make this check daily at the start of the shift.

Check the appropriate box if the item is OK. If there is a problem with the item, leave the space blank and fill out the COMMENTS section below.

Visual Checks	Sun	Mon	Tues	Wed	Thur	Fri	Sat
EXCESS DIRT AND DEBRIS							
DAMAGE (Bent, dented or broken parts, paint transfer)							
LEAKS (Drive unit, brakes, hydraulics)							
TIRES & WHEELS (Drive wheels, load wheels, casters)							
FORKS (In place, properly secured, locking pins)							
CHAINS, CABLES, HOSES (In place)							
GUAGES (Operating)							
PROPANE BOTLE (relief valve, safety strap, fuel level, listen for leaks)							
ENGINE COMPARTMENT (oil, fan belt, battery, etc...)							
GUARDS (Overhead, load backrest, mast, etc.)							
SAFETY DEVICES (<u>Lights</u>, labels, seatbelt, harness, tether)							
MAST ASSEMBLY (no broken welds, no dents)							
Operational Checks	**REPORT ALL UNSAFE CONDITIONS**						
HORN (Sounds)							
STEERING (No binding, no excessive play)							
TRAVEL CONTROLS (All speed ranges, forward/reverse, etc.)							
HYDRAULIC CONTROLS (Raise & lover, tilt forward & back)							
BRAKES (Stop truck within required distance)							
PARKING BRAKE (Seat, hand, foot)							
POWER DISCONNECT (Cuts off all electric power)							
ATTACHMENTS (Function properly)							
EQUIPMENT WAS NOT USED ON THIS PARTICULAR DAY.							
OPERATOR'S INITIALS (PLEASE PRINT CLEARLY)							
Supervisor's Initials upon review:_____							

COMMENTS: (Items needing repair or adjustment)

Date:	Issue:
Resolved Date:	**Resolved By:**
COMMENTS	

CAUTION: If the equipment is found to be in need of repair or in any way unsafe, or contributes to an unsafe condition, the matter shall be reported immediately to the designated authority and the equipment shall not be operated until it has been restored to safe condition. Do not make repairs or adjustments unless specifically authorized to do so.

- Look out for any leaks, cracks, or visible defects in hydraulic hoses or tension in mast chains. – Checking for wet spots around hoses is how to identify hydraulic leaks, look visually around the hose connectors for cracks and bulges. Check along loop points for cracks, bulges, and frayed spots.

- Check fork condition including the top clip retaining pin and heel. – Forks should be able to be moved. Also inspect the tips of the forks, for curling or cracking.

- Check the load backrest extension and see if finger guards are attached. – Load backrest should be free from dents, deflections, or damage.

- Propane connectors for frayed tube or leaking connections. – propane connectors can become damaged over time, so visually inspect the cables and connectors for fraying on the cable and cracks or leaks on the connectors.

- Check if the **accelerator** or direction control pedal is working smoothly. – Inspect these as an operation test, by slowly moving the equipment.

- Tilt control: forward and back should be checked for smooth functioning. – Tilt the mast forward and back, quickly to verify operation is smooth and responsive.

Week Ending: _____

The equipment operator must make this check daily at the start of the shift.

Check the appropriate box if the item is OK. If there is a problem with the item, leave the space blank and fill out the COMMENTS section below.

Visual Checks	Sun	Mon	Tues	Wed	Thur	Fri	Sat
EXCESS DIRT AND DEBRIS							
DAMAGE (Bent, dented or broken parts, paint transfer)							
LEAKS (Drive unit, brakes, hydraulics)							
TIRES & WHEELS (Drive wheels, load wheels, casters)							
FORKS (In place, properly secured, locking pins)							
CHAINS, CABLES, HOSES (In place)							
GUAGES (Operating)							
PROPANE BOTLE (relief valve, safety strap, fuel level, listen for leaks)							
ENGINE COMPARTMENT (oil, fan belt, battery, etc…)							
GUARDS (Overhead, load backrest, mast, etc.)							
SAFETY DEVICES (<u>Lights</u>, labels, seatbelt, harness, tether)							
MAST ASSEMBLY (no broken welds, no dents)							
Operational Checks	_ REPORT ALL UNSAFE CONDITIONS						
HORN (Sounds)							
STEERING (No binding, no excessive play)							
TRAVEL CONTROLS (All speed ranges, forward/reverse, etc.)							
HYDRAULIC CONTROLS (Raise & lover, tilt forward & back)							
BRAKES (Stop truck within required distance)							
PARKING BRAKE (Seat, hand, foot)							
POWER DISCONNECT (Cuts off all electric power)							
ATTACHMENTS (Function properly)							
EQUIPMENT WAS NOT USED ON THIS PARTICULAR DAY.							
OPERATOR'S INITIALS (PLEASE PRINT CLEARLY)							
Supervisor's Initials upon review:_____							

COMMENTS: (Items needing repair or adjustment)

Date:	Issue:
Resolved Date:	**Resolved By:**
COMMENTS	

CAUTION: If the equipment is found to be in need of repair or in any way unsafe, or contributes to an unsafe condition, the matter shall be reported immediately to the designated authority and the equipment shall not be operated until it has been restored to safe condition. Do not make repairs or adjustments unless specifically authorized to do so.

- Inspect tire condition:
    - Pneumatic(air filled) wheels should have pressure and now have cracks through the rubber.
    - Solid wheels should not have large cracks or gouges in them.

- Check for grease and debris in the operator compartment – this can contribute to slipping off the equipment, and cause a serious injury.

- Hood & panel latches – Does the hood and any removable side panels secure in place to no avoid opening or falling off.

- Steering should function smoothly – while testing this, ensure the steering wheel solidly reacts to movements. This should always be monitored during operation.

- Check the functioning of horn and lights – this test is as simple as ensuring the lights aren't burnt out, and the horn operates.

- Back-up alarm (if equipped) should be checked – A backup alarm is a helpful piece of safety equipment. If equipped it must be operational, and not covered in any sound dampening material.

Week Ending: _____

The equipment operator must make this check daily at the start of the shift.

Check the appropriate box if the item is OK. If there is a problem with the item, leave the space blank and fill out the COMMENTS section below.

Visual Checks	Sun	Mon	Tues	Wed	Thur	Fri	Sat
EXCESS DIRT AND DEBRIS							
DAMAGE (Bent, dented or broken parts, paint transfer)							
LEAKS (Drive unit, brakes, hydraulics)							
TIRES & WHEELS (Drive wheels, load wheels, casters)							
FORKS (In place, properly secured, locking pins)							
CHAINS, CABLES, HOSES (In place)							
GUAGES (Operating)							
PROPANE BOTLE (relief valve, safety strap, fuel level, listen for leaks)							
ENGINE COMPARTMENT (oil, fan belt, battery, etc…)							
GUARDS (Overhead, load backrest, mast, etc.)							
SAFETY DEVICES (<u>Lights</u>, labels, seatbelt, harness, tether)							
MAST ASSEMBLY (no broken welds, no dents)							
Operational Checks	**REPORT ALL UNSAFE CONDITIONS**						
HORN (Sounds)							
STEERING (No binding, no excessive play)							
TRAVEL CONTROLS (All speed ranges, forward/reverse, etc.)							
HYDRAULIC CONTROLS (Raise & lover, tilt forward & back)							
BRAKES (Stop truck within required distance)							
PARKING BRAKE (Seat, hand, foot)							
POWER DISCONNECT (Cuts off all electric power)							
ATTACHMENTS (Function properly)							
EQUIPMENT WAS NOT USED ON THIS PARTICULAR DAY.							
OPERATOR'S INITIALS (PLEASE PRINT CLEARLY)							

Supervisor's Initials upon review:_____

COMMENTS: (Items needing repair or adjustment)

Date:	Issue:
Resolved Date:	**Resolved By:**
COMMENTS	

CAUTION: If the equipment is found to be in need of repair or in any way unsafe, or contributes to an unsafe condition, the matter shall be reported immediately to the designated authority and the equipment shall not be operated until it has been restored to safe condition. Do not make repairs or adjustments unless specifically authorized to do so.

- Verify that all safety devices like the seat belt is in proper working condition – The seatbelt should be checked to ensure it locks on quick stops, and that it securely closes.

- Propane bottle restraints – The propane bottle should be secured in place with restraints, which must be locked in place.

- Propane level and connections – Check the level of the propane and the connection points, to ensure you have plenty of fuel for the safe operation and that it isn't leaking.

- Drive control - forward and reverse should be checked for smooth functioning.

- Hoist and lowering control should function smoothly – Check this by raising and lowering the mast, also at this point check the chain, to make sure it has adequate tension.

- Gauges: Functioning of Amp meter, engine oil pressure, Hour Meter, fuel level, temperature, and instrument monitors.

Week Ending: _____

The equipment operator must make this check daily at the start of the shift.

Check the appropriate box if the item is OK. If there is a problem with the item, leave the space blank and fill out the COMMENTS section below.

Visual Checks	Sun	Mon	Tues	Wed	Thur	Fri	Sat
EXCESS DIRT AND DEBRIS							
DAMAGE (Bent, dented or broken parts, paint transfer)							
LEAKS (Drive unit, brakes, hydraulics)							
TIRES & WHEELS (Drive wheels, load wheels, casters)							
FORKS (In place, properly secured, locking pins)							
CHAINS, CABLES, HOSES (In place)							
GUAGES (Operating)							
PROPANE BOTLE (relief valve, safety strap, fuel level, listen for leaks)							
ENGINE COMPARTMENT (oil, fan belt, battery, etc...)							
GUARDS (Overhead, load backrest, mast, etc.)							
SAFETY DEVICES (<u>Lights</u>, labels, seatbelt, harness, tether)							
MAST ASSEMBLY (no broken welds, no dents)							
Operational Checks	REPORT ALL UNSAFE CONDITIONS						
HORN (Sounds)							
STEERING (No binding, no excessive play)							
TRAVEL CONTROLS (All speed ranges, forward/reverse, etc.)							
HYDRAULIC CONTROLS (Raise & lover, tilt forward & back)							
BRAKES (Stop truck within required distance)							
PARKING BRAKE (Seat, hand, foot)							
POWER DISCONNECT (Cuts off all electric power)							
ATTACHMENTS (Function properly)							
EQUIPMENT WAS NOT USED ON THIS PARTICULAR DAY.							
OPERATOR'S INITIALS (PLEASE PRINT CLEARLY)							
Supervisor's Initials upon review:_____							

COMMENTS: (Items needing repair or adjustment)

Date:	Issue:
Resolved Date:	**Resolved By:**
COMMENTS	

CAUTION: If the equipment is found to be in need of repair or in any way unsafe, or contributes to an unsafe condition, the matter shall be reported immediately to the designated authority and the equipment shall not be operated until it has been restored to safe condition. Do not make repairs or adjustments unless specifically authorized to do so.

- Inspect tire condition:
    - Pneumatic(air filled) wheels should have pressure and now have cracks through the rubber.
    - Solid wheels should not have large cracks or gouges in them.

- Check for grease and debris in the operator compartment – this can contribute to slipping off the equipment, and cause a serious injury.

- Hood & panel latches – Does the hood and any removable side panels secure in place to no avoid opening or falling off.

- Steering should function smoothly – while testing this, ensure the steering wheel solidly reacts to movements. This should always be monitored during operation.

- Check the functioning of horn and lights – this test is as simple as ensuring the lights aren't burnt out, and the horn operates.

- Back-up alarm (if equipped) should be checked – A backup alarm is a helpful piece of safety equipment. If equipped it must be operational, and not covered in any sound dampening material.

Week Ending: _____

The equipment operator must make this check daily at the start of the shift.

Check the appropriate box if the item is OK. If there is a problem with the item, leave the space blank and fill out the COMMENTS section below.

Visual Checks	Sun	Mon	Tues	Wed	Thur	Fri	Sat
EXCESS DIRT AND DEBRIS							
DAMAGE (Bent, dented or broken parts, paint transfer)							
LEAKS (Drive unit, brakes, hydraulics)							
TIRES & WHEELS (Drive wheels, load wheels, casters)							
FORKS (In place, properly secured, locking pins)							
CHAINS, CABLES, HOSES (In place)							
GUAGES (Operating)							
PROPANE BOTLE (relief valve, safety strap, fuel level, listen for leaks)							
ENGINE COMPARTMENT (oil, fan belt, battery, etc...)							
GUARDS (Overhead, load backrest, mast, etc.)							
SAFETY DEVICES (Lights, labels, seatbelt, harness, tether)							
MAST ASSEMBLY (no broken welds, no dents)							
Operational Checks	REPORT ALL UNSAFE CONDITIONS						
HORN (Sounds)							
STEERING (No binding, no excessive play)							
TRAVEL CONTROLS (All speed ranges, forward/reverse, etc.)							
HYDRAULIC CONTROLS (Raise & lover, tilt forward & back)							
BRAKES (Stop truck within required distance)							
PARKING BRAKE (Seat, hand, foot)							
POWER DISCONNECT (Cuts off all electric power)							
ATTACHMENTS (Function properly)							
EQUIPMENT WAS NOT USED ON THIS PARTICULAR DAY.							
OPERATOR'S INITIALS (PLEASE PRINT CLEARLY)							
Supervisor's Initials upon review:_____							

COMMENTS: (Items needing repair or adjustment)

Date:	Issue:
Resolved Date:	**Resolved By:**
COMMENTS	

CAUTION: If the equipment is found to be in need of repair or in any way unsafe, or contributes to an unsafe condition, the matter shall be reported immediately to the designated authority and the equipment shall not be operated until it has been restored to safe condition. Do not make repairs or adjustments unless specifically authorized to do so.

- Look out for any leaks, cracks, or visible defects in hydraulic hoses or tension in mast chains. – Checking for wet spots around hoses is how to identify hydraulic leaks, look visually around the hose connectors for cracks and bulges. Check along loop points for cracks, bulges, and frayed spots.

- Check fork condition including the top clip retaining pin and heel. – Forks should be able to be moved. Also inspect the tips of the forks, for curling or cracking.

- Check the load backrest extension and see if finger guards are attached. – Load backrest should be free from dents, deflections, or damage.

- Propane connectors for frayed tube or leaking connections. – propane connectors can become damaged over time, so visually inspect the cables and connectors for fraying on the cable and cracks or leaks on the connectors.

- Check if the **accelerator** or direction control pedal is working smoothly. – Inspect these as an operation test, by slowly moving the equipment.

- Tilt control: forward and back should be checked for smooth functioning. – Tilt the mast forward and back, quickly to verify operation is smooth and responsive.

Week Ending: _____

The equipment operator must make this check daily at the start of the shift.

Check the appropriate box if the item is OK. If there is a problem with the item, leave the space blank and fill out the COMMENTS section below.

Visual Checks	Sun	Mon	Tues	Wed	Thur	Fri	Sat
EXCESS DIRT AND DEBRIS							
DAMAGE (Bent, dented or broken parts, paint transfer)							
LEAKS (Drive unit, brakes, hydraulics)							
TIRES & WHEELS (Drive wheels, load wheels, casters)							
FORKS (In place, properly secured, locking pins)							
CHAINS, CABLES, HOSES (In place)							
GUAGES (Operating)							
PROPANE BOTLE (relief valve, safety strap, fuel level, listen for leaks)							
ENGINE COMPARTMENT (oil, fan belt, battery, etc…)							
GUARDS (Overhead, load backrest, mast, etc.)							
SAFETY DEVICES (<u>Lights</u>, labels, seatbelt, harness, tether)							
MAST ASSEMBLY (no broken welds, no dents)							
Operational Checks	REPORT ALL UNSAFE CONDITIONS						
HORN (Sounds)							
STEERING (No binding, no excessive play)							
TRAVEL CONTROLS (All speed ranges, forward/reverse, etc.)							
HYDRAULIC CONTROLS (Raise & lover, tilt forward & back)							
BRAKES (Stop truck within required distance)							
PARKING BRAKE (Seat, hand, foot)							
POWER DISCONNECT (Cuts off all electric power)							
ATTACHMENTS (Function properly)							
EQUIPMENT WAS NOT USED ON THIS PARTICULAR DAY.							
OPERATOR'S INITIALS (PLEASE PRINT CLEARLY)							

Supervisor's Initials upon review:_____

COMMENTS: (Items needing repair or adjustment)

Date:	Issue:
Resolved Date:	**Resolved By:**
COMMENTS	

CAUTION: If the equipment is found to be in need of repair or in any way unsafe, or contributes to an unsafe condition, the matter shall be reported immediately to the designated authority and the equipment shall not be operated until it has been restored to safe condition. Do not make repairs or adjustments unless specifically authorized to do so.

- Inspect tire condition:
  - Pneumatic(air filled) wheels should have pressure and now have cracks through the rubber.
  - Solid wheels should not have large cracks or gouges in them.

- Check for grease and debris in the operator compartment – this can contribute to slipping off the equipment, and cause a serious injury.

- Hood & panel latches – Does the hood and any removable side panels secure in place to no avoid opening or falling off.

- Steering should function smoothly – while testing this, ensure the steering wheel solidly reacts to movements. This should always be monitored during operation.

- Check the functioning of horn and lights – this test is as simple as ensuring the lights aren't burnt out, and the horn operates.

- Back-up alarm (if equipped) should be checked – A backup alarm is a helpful piece of safety equipment. If equipped it must be operational, and not covered in any sound dampening material.

Week Ending: _____

The equipment operator must make this check daily at the start of the shift.

Check the appropriate box if the item is OK. If there is a problem with the item, leave the space blank and fill out the COMMENTS section below.

Visual Checks	Sun	Mon	Tues	Wed	Thur	Fri	Sat
EXCESS DIRT AND DEBRIS							
DAMAGE (Bent, dented or broken parts, paint transfer)							
LEAKS (Drive unit, brakes, hydraulics)							
TIRES & WHEELS (Drive wheels, load wheels, casters)							
FORKS (In place, properly secured, locking pins)							
CHAINS, CABLES, HOSES (In place)							
GUAGES (Operating)							
PROPANE BOTLE (relief valve, safety strap, fuel level, listen for leaks)							
ENGINE COMPARTMENT (oil, fan belt, battery, etc…)							
GUARDS (Overhead, load backrest, mast, etc.)							
SAFETY DEVICES (<u>Lights</u>, labels, seatbelt, harness, tether)							
MAST ASSEMBLY (no broken welds, no dents)							
Operational Checks	REPORT ALL UNSAFE CONDITIONS						
HORN (Sounds)							
STEERING (No binding, no excessive play)							
TRAVEL CONTROLS (All speed ranges, forward/reverse, etc.)							
HYDRAULIC CONTROLS (Raise & lover, tilt forward & back)							
BRAKES (Stop truck within required distance)							
PARKING BRAKE (Seat, hand, foot)							
POWER DISCONNECT (Cuts off all electric power)							
ATTACHMENTS (Function properly)							
EQUIPMENT WAS NOT USED ON THIS PARTICULAR DAY.							
OPERATOR'S INITIALS (PLEASE PRINT CLEARLY)							
Supervisor's Initials upon review:_____							

COMMENTS: (Items needing repair or adjustment)

Date:	Issue:
Resolved Date:	Resolved By:
COMMENTS	

CAUTION: If the equipment is found to be in need of repair or in any way unsafe, or contributes to an unsafe condition, the matter shall be reported immediately to the designated authority and the equipment shall not be operated until it has been restored to safe condition. Do not make repairs or adjustments unless specifically authorized to do so.

- Verify that all safety devices like the seat belt is in proper working condition – The seatbelt should be checked to ensure it locks on quick stops, and that it securely closes.

- Propane bottle restraints – The propane bottle should be secured in place with restraints, which must be locked in place.

- Propane level and connections – Check the level of the propane and the connection points, to ensure you have plenty of fuel for the safe operation and that it isn't leaking.

- Drive control - forward and reverse should be checked for smooth functioning.

- Hoist and lowering control should function smoothly – Check this by raising and lowering the mast, also at this point check the chain, to make sure it has adequate tension.

- Gauges: Functioning of Amp meter, engine oil pressure, Hour Meter, fuel level, temperature, and instrument monitors.

Week Ending: _____

The equipment operator must make this check daily at the start of the shift.

Check the appropriate box if the item is OK. If there is a problem with the item, leave the space blank and fill out the COMMENTS section below.

Visual Checks	Sun	Mon	Tues	Wed	Thur	Fri	Sat
EXCESS DIRT AND DEBRIS							
DAMAGE (Bent, dented or broken parts, paint transfer)							
LEAKS (Drive unit, brakes, hydraulics)							
TIRES & WHEELS (Drive wheels, load wheels, casters)							
FORKS (In place, properly secured, locking pins)							
CHAINS, CABLES, HOSES (In place)							
GUAGES (Operating)							
PROPANE BOTLE (relief valve, safety strap, fuel level, listen for leaks)							
ENGINE COMPARTMENT (oil, fan belt, battery, etc…)							
GUARDS (Overhead, load backrest, mast, etc.)							
SAFETY DEVICES (<u>Lights</u>, labels, seatbelt, harness, tether)							
MAST ASSEMBLY (no broken welds, no dents)							
Operational Checks	**REPORT ALL UNSAFE CONDITIONS**						
HORN (Sounds)							
STEERING (No binding, no excessive play)							
TRAVEL CONTROLS (All speed ranges, forward/reverse, etc.)							
HYDRAULIC CONTROLS (Raise & lover, tilt forward & back)							
BRAKES (Stop truck within required distance)							
PARKING BRAKE (Seat, hand, foot)							
POWER DISCONNECT (Cuts off all electric power)							
ATTACHMENTS (Function properly)							
EQUIPMENT WAS NOT USED ON THIS PARTICULAR DAY.							
OPERATOR'S INITIALS (PLEASE PRINT CLEARLY)							

Supervisor's Initials upon review:_____

COMMENTS: (Items needing repair or adjustment)

Date:	Issue:
Resolved Date:	**Resolved By:**
COMMENTS	

CAUTION: If the equipment is found to be in need of repair or in any way unsafe, or contributes to an unsafe condition, the matter shall be reported immediately to the designated authority and the equipment shall not be operated until it has been restored to safe condition. Do not make repairs or adjustments unless specifically authorized to do so.

- Inspect tire condition:
  - Pneumatic(air filled) wheels should have pressure and now have cracks through the rubber.
  - Solid wheels should not have large cracks or gouges in them.

- Check for grease and debris in the operator compartment – this can contribute to slipping off the equipment, and cause a serious injury.

- Hood & panel latches – Does the hood and any removable side panels secure in place to no avoid opening or falling off.

- Steering should function smoothly – while testing this, ensure the steering wheel solidly reacts to movements. This should always be monitored during operation.

- Check the functioning of horn and lights – this test is as simple as ensuring the lights aren't burnt out, and the horn operates.

- Back-up alarm (if equipped) should be checked – A backup alarm is a helpful piece of safety equipment. If equipped it must be operational, and not covered in any sound dampening material.

Week Ending: _____							
The equipment operator must make this check daily at the start of the shift.							
Check the appropriate box if the item is OK. If there is a problem with the item, leave the space blank and fill out the COMMENTS section below.							

Visual Checks	Sun	Mon	Tues	Wed	Thur	Fri	Sat
EXCESS DIRT AND DEBRIS							
DAMAGE (Bent, dented or broken parts, paint transfer)							
LEAKS (Drive unit, brakes, hydraulics)							
TIRES & WHEELS (Drive wheels, load wheels, casters)							
FORKS (In place, properly secured, locking pins)							
CHAINS, CABLES, HOSES (In place)							
GUAGES (Operating)							
PROPANE BOTLE (relief valve, safety strap, fuel level, listen for leaks)							
ENGINE COMPARTMENT (oil, fan belt, battery, etc…)							
GUARDS (Overhead, load backrest, mast, etc.)							
SAFETY DEVICES (<u>Lights</u>, labels, seatbelt, harness, tether)							
MAST ASSEMBLY (no broken welds, no dents)							
Operational Checks	**REPORT ALL UNSAFE CONDITIONS**						
HORN (Sounds)							
STEERING (No binding, no excessive play)							
TRAVEL CONTROLS (All speed ranges, forward/reverse, etc.)							
HYDRAULIC CONTROLS (Raise & lover, tilt forward & back)							
BRAKES (Stop truck within required distance)							
PARKING BRAKE (Seat, hand, foot)							
POWER DISCONNECT (Cuts off all electric power)							
ATTACHMENTS (Function properly)							
EQUIPMENT WAS NOT USED ON THIS PARTICULAR DAY.							
OPERATOR'S INITIALS (PLEASE PRINT CLEARLY)							
Supervisor's Initials upon review:_____							

COMMENTS: (Items needing repair or adjustment)

Date:	Issue:
Resolved Date:	**Resolved By:**
COMMENTS	

CAUTION: If the equipment is found to be in need of repair or in any way unsafe, or contributes to an unsafe condition, the matter shall be reported immediately to the designated authority and the equipment shall not be operated until it has been restored to safe condition. Do not make repairs or adjustments unless specifically authorized to do so.

- Look out for any leaks, cracks, or visible defects in hydraulic hoses or tension in mast chains. – Checking for wet spots around hoses is how to identify hydraulic leaks, look visually around the hose connectors for cracks and bulges. Check along loop points for cracks, bulges, and frayed spots.

- Check fork condition including the top clip retaining pin and heel. – Forks should be able to be moved. Also inspect the tips of the forks, for curling or cracking.

- Check the load backrest extension and see if finger guards are attached. – Load backrest should be free from dents, deflections, or damage.

- Propane connectors for frayed tube or leaking connections. – propane connectors can become damaged over time, so visually inspect the cables and connectors for fraying on the cable and cracks or leaks on the connectors.

- Check if the **accelerator** or direction control pedal is working smoothly. – Inspect these as an operation test, by slowly moving the equipment.

- Tilt control: forward and back should be checked for smooth functioning. – Tilt the mast forward and back, quickly to verify operation is smooth and responsive.

Week Ending: _____

The equipment operator must make this check daily at the start of the shift.

Check the appropriate box if the item is OK. If there is a problem with the item, leave the space blank and fill out the COMMENTS section below.

Visual Checks	Sun	Mon	Tues	Wed	Thur	Fri	Sat
EXCESS DIRT AND DEBRIS							
DAMAGE (Bent, dented or broken parts, paint transfer)							
LEAKS (Drive unit, brakes, hydraulics)							
TIRES & WHEELS (Drive wheels, load wheels, casters)							
FORKS (In place, properly secured, locking pins)							
CHAINS, CABLES, HOSES (In place)							
GUAGES (Operating)							
PROPANE BOTLE (relief valve, safety strap, fuel level, listen for leaks)							
ENGINE COMPARTMENT (oil, fan belt, battery, etc...)							
GUARDS (Overhead, load backrest, mast, etc.)							
SAFETY DEVICES (<u>Lights</u>, labels, seatbelt, harness, tether)							
MAST ASSEMBLY (no broken welds, no dents)							
Operational Checks		**REPORT ALL UNSAFE CONDITIONS**					
HORN (Sounds)							
STEERING (No binding, no excessive play)							
TRAVEL CONTROLS (All speed ranges, forward/reverse, etc.)							
HYDRAULIC CONTROLS (Raise & lover, tilt forward & back)							
BRAKES (Stop truck within required distance)							
PARKING BRAKE (Seat, hand, foot)							
POWER DISCONNECT (Cuts off all electric power)							
ATTACHMENTS (Function properly)							
EQUIPMENT WAS NOT USED ON THIS PARTICULAR DAY.							
OPERATOR'S INITIALS (PLEASE PRINT CLEARLY)							

Supervisor's Initials upon review:_____

COMMENTS: (Items needing repair or adjustment)

Date:	Issue:
Resolved Date:	**Resolved By:**
COMMENTS	

CAUTION: If the equipment is found to be in need of repair or in any way unsafe, or contributes to an unsafe condition, the matter shall be reported immediately to the designated authority and the equipment shall not be operated until it has been restored to safe condition. Do not make repairs or adjustments unless specifically authorized to do so.

- Inspect tire condition:
  - Pneumatic(air filled) wheels should have pressure and now have cracks through the rubber.
  - Solid wheels should not have large cracks or gouges in them.

- Check for grease and debris in the operator compartment – this can contribute to slipping off the equipment, and cause a serious injury.

- Hood & panel latches – Does the hood and any removable side panels secure in place to no avoid opening or falling off.

- Steering should function smoothly – while testing this, ensure the steering wheel solidly reacts to movements. This should always be monitored during operation.

- Check the functioning of horn and lights – this test is as simple as ensuring the lights aren't burnt out, and the horn operates.

- Back-up alarm (if equipped) should be checked – A backup alarm is a helpful piece of safety equipment. If equipped it must be operational, and not covered in any sound dampening material.

Week Ending: _____

The equipment operator must make this check daily at the start of the shift.

Check the appropriate box if the item is OK. If there is a problem with the item, leave the space blank and fill out the COMMENTS section below.

Visual Checks	Sun	Mon	Tues	Wed	Thur	Fri	Sat
EXCESS DIRT AND DEBRIS							
DAMAGE (Bent, dented or broken parts, paint transfer)							
LEAKS (Drive unit, brakes, hydraulics)							
TIRES & WHEELS (Drive wheels, load wheels, casters)							
FORKS (In place, properly secured, locking pins)							
CHAINS, CABLES, HOSES (In place)							
GUAGES (Operating)							
PROPANE BOTLE (relief valve, safety strap, fuel level, listen for leaks)							
ENGINE COMPARTMENT (oil, fan belt, battery, etc...)							
GUARDS (Overhead, load backrest, mast, etc.)							
SAFETY DEVICES (<u>Lights</u>, labels, seatbelt, harness, tether)							
MAST ASSEMBLY (no broken welds, no dents)							
Operational Checks	REPORT ALL UNSAFE CONDITIONS						
HORN (Sounds)							
STEERING (No binding, no excessive play)							
TRAVEL CONTROLS (All speed ranges, forward/reverse, etc.)							
HYDRAULIC CONTROLS (Raise & lover, tilt forward & back)							
BRAKES (Stop truck within required distance)							
PARKING BRAKE (Seat, hand, foot)							
POWER DISCONNECT (Cuts off all electric power)							
ATTACHMENTS (Function properly)							
EQUIPMENT WAS NOT USED ON THIS PARTICULAR DAY.							
OPERATOR'S INITIALS (PLEASE PRINT CLEARLY)							

Supervisor's Initials upon review:_____

COMMENTS: (Items needing repair or adjustment)

Date:	Issue:
Resolved Date:	**Resolved By:**

COMMENTS

CAUTION: If the equipment is found to be in need of repair or in any way unsafe, or contributes to an unsafe condition, the matter shall be reported immediately to the designated authority and the equipment shall not be operated until it has been restored to safe condition. Do not make repairs or adjustments unless specifically authorized to do so.

- Verify that all safety devices like the seat belt is in proper working condition – The seatbelt should be checked to ensure it locks on quick stops, and that it securely closes.

- Propane bottle restraints – The propane bottle should be secured in place with restraints, which must be locked in place.

- Propane level and connections – Check the level of the propane and the connection points, to ensure you have plenty of fuel for the safe operation and that it isn't leaking.

- Drive control - forward and reverse should be checked for smooth functioning.

- Hoist and lowering control should function smoothly – Check this by raising and lowering the mast, also at this point check the chain, to make sure it has adequate tension.

- Gauges: Functioning of Amp meter, engine oil pressure, Hour Meter, fuel level, temperature, and instrument monitors.

Week Ending: _____
The equipment operator must make this check daily at the start of the shift.
Check the appropriate box if the item is OK. If there is a problem with the item, leave the space blank and fill out the COMMENTS section below.

Visual Checks	Sun	Mon	Tues	Wed	Thur	Fri	Sat
EXCESS DIRT AND DEBRIS							
DAMAGE (Bent, dented or broken parts, paint transfer)							
LEAKS (Drive unit, brakes, hydraulics)							
TIRES & WHEELS (Drive wheels, load wheels, casters)							
FORKS (In place, properly secured, locking pins)							
CHAINS, CABLES, HOSES (In place)							
GUAGES (Operating)							
PROPANE BOTLE (relief valve, safety strap, fuel level, listen for leaks)							
ENGINE COMPARTMENT (oil, fan belt, battery, etc…)							
GUARDS (Overhead, load backrest, mast, etc.)							
SAFETY DEVICES (Lights, labels, seatbelt, harness, tether)							
MAST ASSEMBLY (no broken welds, no dents)							
Operational Checks	**REPORT ALL UNSAFE CONDITIONS**						
HORN (Sounds)							
STEERING (No binding, no excessive play)							
TRAVEL CONTROLS (All speed ranges, forward/reverse, etc.)							
HYDRAULIC CONTROLS (Raise & lover, tilt forward & back)							
BRAKES (Stop truck within required distance)							
PARKING BRAKE (Seat, hand, foot)							
POWER DISCONNECT (Cuts off all electric power)							
ATTACHMENTS (Function properly)							
EQUIPMENT WAS NOT USED ON THIS PARTICULAR DAY.							
OPERATOR'S INITIALS (PLEASE PRINT CLEARLY)							
Supervisor's Initials upon review:_____							

COMMENTS: (Items needing repair or adjustment)

Date:	Issue:
Resolved Date:	**Resolved By:**
COMMENTS	

CAUTION: If the equipment is found to be in need of repair or in any way unsafe, or contributes to an unsafe condition, the matter shall be reported immediately to the designated authority and the equipment shall not be operated until it has been restored to safe condition. Do not make repairs or adjustments unless specifically authorized to do so.

- Inspect tire condition:
  - Pneumatic(air filled) wheels should have pressure and now have cracks through the rubber.
  - Solid wheels should not have large cracks or gouges in them.

- Check for grease and debris in the operator compartment – this can contribute to slipping off the equipment, and cause a serious injury.

- Hood & panel latches – Does the hood and any removable side panels secure in place to no avoid opening or falling off.

- Steering should function smoothly – while testing this, ensure the steering wheel solidly reacts to movements. This should always be monitored during operation.

- Check the functioning of horn and lights – this test is as simple as ensuring the lights aren't burnt out, and the horn operates.

- Back-up alarm (if equipped) should be checked – A backup alarm is a helpful piece of safety equipment. If equipped it must be operational, and not covered in any sound dampening material.

Week Ending: _____

The equipment operator must make this check daily at the start of the shift.

Check the appropriate box if the item is OK. If there is a problem with the item, leave the space blank and fill out the COMMENTS section below.

Visual Checks	Sun	Mon	Tues	Wed	Thur	Fri	Sat
EXCESS DIRT AND DEBRIS							
DAMAGE (Bent, dented or broken parts, paint transfer)							
LEAKS (Drive unit, brakes, hydraulics)							
TIRES & WHEELS (Drive wheels, load wheels, casters)							
FORKS (In place, properly secured, locking pins)							
CHAINS, CABLES, HOSES (In place)							
GUAGES (Operating)							
PROPANE BOTLE (relief valve, safety strap, fuel level, listen for leaks)							
ENGINE COMPARTMENT (oil, fan belt, battery, etc…)							
GUARDS (Overhead, load backrest, mast, etc.)							
SAFETY DEVICES (<u>Lights</u>, labels, seatbelt, harness, tether)							
MAST ASSEMBLY (no broken welds, no dents)							
Operational Checks	**REPORT ALL UNSAFE CONDITIONS**						
HORN (Sounds)							
STEERING (No binding, no excessive play)							
TRAVEL CONTROLS (All speed ranges, forward/reverse, etc.)							
HYDRAULIC CONTROLS (Raise & lover, tilt forward & back)							
BRAKES (Stop truck within required distance)							
PARKING BRAKE (Seat, hand, foot)							
POWER DISCONNECT (Cuts off all electric power)							
ATTACHMENTS (Function properly)							
EQUIPMENT WAS NOT USED ON THIS PARTICULAR DAY.							
OPERATOR'S INITIALS (PLEASE PRINT CLEARLY)							

Supervisor's Initials upon review:_____

COMMENTS: (Items needing repair or adjustment)

Date:	Issue:
Resolved Date:	**Resolved By:**
COMMENTS	

CAUTION: If the equipment is found to be in need of repair or in any way unsafe, or contributes to an unsafe condition, the matter shall be reported immediately to the designated authority and the equipment shall not be operated until it has been restored to safe condition. Do not make repairs or adjustments unless specifically authorized to do so.

- Look out for any leaks, cracks, or visible defects in hydraulic hoses or tension in mast chains. – Checking for wet spots around hoses is how to identify hydraulic leaks, look visually around the hose connectors for cracks and bulges. Check along loop points for cracks, bulges, and frayed spots.

- Check fork condition including the top clip retaining pin and heel. – Forks should be able to be moved. Also inspect the tips of the forks, for curling or cracking.

- Check the load backrest extension and see if finger guards are attached. – Load backrest should be free from dents, deflections, or damage.

- Propane connectors for frayed tube or leaking connections. – propane connectors can become damaged over time, so visually inspect the cables and connectors for fraying on the cable and cracks or leaks on the connectors.

- Check if the **accelerator** or direction control pedal is working smoothly. – Inspect these as an operation test, by slowly moving the equipment.

- Tilt control: forward and back should be checked for smooth functioning. – Tilt the mast forward and back, quickly to verify operation is smooth and responsive.

Week Ending: _____

The equipment operator must make this check daily at the start of the shift.

Check the appropriate box if the item is OK. If there is a problem with the item, leave the space blank and fill out the COMMENTS section below.

Visual Checks	Sun	Mon	Tues	Wed	Thur	Fri	Sat
EXCESS DIRT AND DEBRIS							
DAMAGE (Bent, dented or broken parts, paint transfer)							
LEAKS (Drive unit, brakes, hydraulics)							
TIRES & WHEELS (Drive wheels, load wheels, casters)							
FORKS (In place, properly secured, locking pins)							
CHAINS, CABLES, HOSES (In place)							
GUAGES (Operating)							
PROPANE BOTLE (relief valve, safety strap, fuel level, listen for leaks)							
ENGINE COMPARTMENT (oil, fan belt, battery, etc…)							
GUARDS (Overhead, load backrest, mast, etc.)							
SAFETY DEVICES (Lights, labels, seatbelt, harness, tether)							
MAST ASSEMBLY (no broken welds, no dents)							
Operational Checks	REPORT ALL UNSAFE CONDITIONS						
HORN (Sounds)							
STEERING (No binding, no excessive play)							
TRAVEL CONTROLS (All speed ranges, forward/reverse, etc.)							
HYDRAULIC CONTROLS (Raise & lover, tilt forward & back)							
BRAKES (Stop truck within required distance)							
PARKING BRAKE (Seat, hand, foot)							
POWER DISCONNECT (Cuts off all electric power)							
ATTACHMENTS (Function properly)							
EQUIPMENT WAS NOT USED ON THIS PARTICULAR DAY.							
OPERATOR'S INITIALS (PLEASE PRINT CLEARLY)							

Supervisor's Initials upon review:_____

COMMENTS: (Items needing repair or adjustment)

Date:	Issue:
Resolved Date:	**Resolved By:**
COMMENTS	

CAUTION: If the equipment is found to be in need of repair or in any way unsafe, or contributes to an unsafe condition, the matter shall be reported immediately to the designated authority and the equipment shall not be operated until it has been restored to safe condition. Do not make repairs or adjustments unless specifically authorized to do so.

- Inspect tire condition:
  - Pneumatic(air filled) wheels should have pressure and now have cracks through the rubber.
  - Solid wheels should not have large cracks or gouges in them.

- Check for grease and debris in the operator compartment – this can contribute to slipping off the equipment, and cause a serious injury.

- Hood & panel latches – Does the hood and any removable side panels secure in place to no avoid opening or falling off.

- Steering should function smoothly – while testing this, ensure the steering wheel solidly reacts to movements. This should always be monitored during operation.

- Check the functioning of horn and lights – this test is as simple as ensuring the lights aren't burnt out, and the horn operates.

- Back-up alarm (if equipped) should be checked – A backup alarm is a helpful piece of safety equipment. If equipped it must be operational, and not covered in any sound dampening material.

Week Ending: _____

The equipment operator must make this check daily at the start of the shift.

Check the appropriate box if the item is OK. If there is a problem with the item, leave the space blank and fill out the COMMENTS section below.

Visual Checks	Sun	Mon	Tues	Wed	Thur	Fri	Sat
EXCESS DIRT AND DEBRIS							
DAMAGE (Bent, dented or broken parts, paint transfer)							
LEAKS (Drive unit, brakes, hydraulics)							
TIRES & WHEELS (Drive wheels, load wheels, casters)							
FORKS (In place, properly secured, locking pins)							
CHAINS, CABLES, HOSES (In place)							
GUAGES (Operating)							
PROPANE BOTLE (relief valve, safety strap, fuel level, listen for leaks)							
ENGINE COMPARTMENT (oil, fan belt, battery, etc…)							
GUARDS (Overhead, load backrest, mast, etc.)							
SAFETY DEVICES (<u>Lights</u>, labels, seatbelt, harness, tether)							
MAST ASSEMBLY (no broken welds, no dents)							
Operational Checks	**REPORT ALL UNSAFE CONDITIONS**						
HORN (Sounds)							
STEERING (No binding, no excessive play)							
TRAVEL CONTROLS (All speed ranges, forward/reverse, etc.)							
HYDRAULIC CONTROLS (Raise & lover, tilt forward & back)							
BRAKES (Stop truck within required distance)							
PARKING BRAKE (Seat, hand, foot)							
POWER DISCONNECT (Cuts off all electric power)							
ATTACHMENTS (Function properly)							
EQUIPMENT WAS NOT USED ON THIS PARTICULAR DAY.							
OPERATOR'S INITIALS (PLEASE PRINT CLEARLY)							
Supervisor's Initials upon review:_____							

COMMENTS: (Items needing repair or adjustment)

Date:	Issue:
Resolved Date:	**Resolved By:**
COMMENTS	

CAUTION: If the equipment is found to be in need of repair or in any way unsafe, or contributes to an unsafe condition, the matter shall be reported immediately to the designated authority and the equipment shall not be operated until it has been restored to safe condition. Do not make repairs or adjustments unless specifically authorized to do so.

- Verify that all safety devices like the seat belt is in proper working condition – The seatbelt should be checked to ensure it locks on quick stops, and that it securely closes.

- Propane bottle restraints – The propane bottle should be secured in place with restraints, which must be locked in place.

- Propane level and connections – Check the level of the propane and the connection points, to ensure you have plenty of fuel for the safe operation and that it isn't leaking.

- Drive control - forward and reverse should be checked for smooth functioning.

- Hoist and lowering control should function smoothly – Check this by raising and lowering the mast, also at this point check the chain, to make sure it has adequate tension.

- Gauges: Functioning of Amp meter, engine oil pressure, Hour Meter, fuel level, temperature, and instrument monitors.

Week Ending: _____

The equipment operator must make this check daily at the start of the shift.

Check the appropriate box if the item is OK. If there is a problem with the item, leave the space blank and fill out the COMMENTS section below.

Visual Checks	Sun	Mon	Tues	Wed	Thur	Fri	Sat
EXCESS DIRT AND DEBRIS							
DAMAGE (Bent, dented or broken parts, paint transfer)							
LEAKS (Drive unit, brakes, hydraulics)							
TIRES & WHEELS (Drive wheels, load wheels, casters)							
FORKS (In place, properly secured, locking pins)							
CHAINS, CABLES, HOSES (In place)							
GUAGES (Operating)							
PROPANE BOTLE (relief valve, safety strap, fuel level, listen for leaks)							
ENGINE COMPARTMENT (oil, fan belt, battery, etc...)							
GUARDS (Overhead, load backrest, mast, etc.)							
SAFETY DEVICES (<u>Lights</u>, labels, seatbelt, harness, tether)							
MAST ASSEMBLY (no broken welds, no dents)							
Operational Checks	REPORT ALL UNSAFE CONDITIONS						
HORN (Sounds)							
STEERING (No binding, no excessive play)							
TRAVEL CONTROLS (All speed ranges, forward/reverse, etc.)							
HYDRAULIC CONTROLS (Raise & lover, tilt forward & back)							
BRAKES (Stop truck within required distance)							
PARKING BRAKE (Seat, hand, foot)							
POWER DISCONNECT (Cuts off all electric power)							
ATTACHMENTS (Function properly)							
EQUIPMENT WAS NOT USED ON THIS PARTICULAR DAY.							
OPERATOR'S INITIALS (PLEASE PRINT CLEARLY)							
Supervisor's Initials upon review:_____							

COMMENTS: (Items needing repair or adjustment)

Date:	Issue:
Resolved Date:	Resolved By:
COMMENTS	

CAUTION: If the equipment is found to be in need of repair or in any way unsafe, or contributes to an unsafe condition, the matter shall be reported immediately to the designated authority and the equipment shall not be operated until it has been restored to safe condition. Do not make repairs or adjustments unless specifically authorized to do so.

- Inspect tire condition:
  - Pneumatic(air filled) wheels should have pressure and now have cracks through the rubber.
  - Solid wheels should not have large cracks or gouges in them.

- Check for grease and debris in the operator compartment – this can contribute to slipping off the equipment, and cause a serious injury.

- Hood & panel latches – Does the hood and any removable side panels secure in place to no avoid opening or falling off.

- Steering should function smoothly – while testing this, ensure the steering wheel solidly reacts to movements. This should always be monitored during operation.

- Check the functioning of horn and lights – this test is as simple as ensuring the lights aren't burnt out, and the horn operates.

- Back-up alarm (if equipped) should be checked – A backup alarm is a helpful piece of safety equipment. If equipped it must be operational, and not covered in any sound dampening material.

Week Ending: _____

The equipment operator must make this check daily at the start of the shift.

Check the appropriate box if the item is OK. If there is a problem with the item, leave the space blank and fill out the COMMENTS section below.

Visual Checks	Sun	Mon	Tues	Wed	Thur	Fri	Sat
EXCESS DIRT AND DEBRIS							
DAMAGE (Bent, dented or broken parts, paint transfer)							
LEAKS (Drive unit, brakes, hydraulics)							
TIRES & WHEELS (Drive wheels, load wheels, casters)							
FORKS (In place, properly secured, locking pins)							
CHAINS, CABLES, HOSES (In place)							
GUAGES (Operating)							
PROPANE BOTLE (relief valve, safety strap, fuel level, listen for leaks)							
ENGINE COMPARTMENT (oil, fan belt, battery, etc…)							
GUARDS (Overhead, load backrest, mast, etc.)							
SAFETY DEVICES (<u>Lights</u>, labels, seatbelt, harness, tether)							
MAST ASSEMBLY (no broken welds, no dents)							
Operational Checks	**REPORT ALL UNSAFE CONDITIONS**						
HORN (Sounds)							
STEERING (No binding, no excessive play)							
TRAVEL CONTROLS (All speed ranges, forward/reverse, etc.)							
HYDRAULIC CONTROLS (Raise & lover, tilt forward & back)							
BRAKES (Stop truck within required distance)							
PARKING BRAKE (Seat, hand, foot)							
POWER DISCONNECT (Cuts off all electric power)							
ATTACHMENTS (Function properly)							
EQUIPMENT WAS NOT USED ON THIS PARTICULAR DAY.							
OPERATOR'S INITIALS (PLEASE PRINT CLEARLY)							
Supervisor's Initials upon review:_____							

COMMENTS: (Items needing repair or adjustment)

Date:	Issue:
Resolved Date:	**Resolved By:**
COMMENTS	

CAUTION: If the equipment is found to be in need of repair or in any way unsafe, or contributes to an unsafe condition, the matter shall be reported immediately to the designated authority and the equipment shall not be operated until it has been restored to safe condition. Do not make repairs or adjustments unless specifically authorized to do so.

- Look out for any leaks, cracks, or visible defects in hydraulic hoses or tension in mast chains. – Checking for wet spots around hoses is how to identify hydraulic leaks, look visually around the hose connectors for cracks and bulges. Check along loop points for cracks, bulges, and frayed spots.

- Check fork condition including the top clip retaining pin and heel. – Forks should be able to be moved. Also inspect the tips of the forks, for curling or cracking.

- Check the load backrest extension and see if finger guards are attached. – Load backrest should be free from dents, deflections, or damage.

- Propane connectors for frayed tube or leaking connections. – propane connectors can become damaged over time, so visually inspect the cables and connectors for fraying on the cable and cracks or leaks on the connectors.

- Check if the **accelerator** or direction control pedal is working smoothly. – Inspect these as an operation test, by slowly moving the equipment.

- Tilt control: forward and back should be checked for smooth functioning. – Tilt the mast forward and back, quickly to verify operation is smooth and responsive.

Week Ending: _____

The equipment operator must make this check daily at the start of the shift.

Check the appropriate box if the item is OK. If there is a problem with the item, leave the space blank and fill out the COMMENTS section below.

Visual Checks	Sun	Mon	Tues	Wed	Thur	Fri	Sat
EXCESS DIRT AND DEBRIS							
DAMAGE (Bent, dented or broken parts, paint transfer)							
LEAKS (Drive unit, brakes, hydraulics)							
TIRES & WHEELS (Drive wheels, load wheels, casters)							
FORKS (In place, properly secured, locking pins)							
CHAINS, CABLES, HOSES (In place)							
GUAGES (Operating)							
PROPANE BOTLE (relief valve, safety strap, fuel level, listen for leaks)							
ENGINE COMPARTMENT (oil, fan belt, battery, etc…)							
GUARDS (Overhead, load backrest, mast, etc.)							
SAFETY DEVICES (<u>Lights</u>, labels, seatbelt, harness, tether)							
MAST ASSEMBLY (no broken welds, no dents)							
Operational Checks			**REPORT ALL UNSAFE CONDITIONS**				
HORN (Sounds)							
STEERING (No binding, no excessive play)							
TRAVEL CONTROLS (All speed ranges, forward/reverse, etc.)							
HYDRAULIC CONTROLS (Raise & lover, tilt forward & back)							
BRAKES (Stop truck within required distance)							
PARKING BRAKE (Seat, hand, foot)							
POWER DISCONNECT (Cuts off all electric power)							
ATTACHMENTS (Function properly)							
EQUIPMENT WAS NOT USED ON THIS PARTICULAR DAY.							
OPERATOR'S INITIALS (PLEASE PRINT CLEARLY)							

Supervisor's Initials upon review:_____

COMMENTS: (Items needing repair or adjustment)

Date:	Issue:
Resolved Date:	**Resolved By:**
COMMENTS	

CAUTION: If the equipment is found to be in need of repair or in any way unsafe, or contributes to an unsafe condition, the matter shall be reported immediately to the designated authority and the equipment shall not be operated until it has been restored to safe condition. Do not make repairs or adjustments unless specifically authorized to do so.

- Inspect tire condition:
  - Pneumatic(air filled) wheels should have pressure and now have cracks through the rubber.
  - Solid wheels should not have large cracks or gouges in them.

- Check for grease and debris in the operator compartment – this can contribute to slipping off the equipment, and cause a serious injury.

- Hood & panel latches – Does the hood and any removable side panels secure in place to no avoid opening or falling off.

- Steering should function smoothly – while testing this, ensure the steering wheel solidly reacts to movements. This should always be monitored during operation.

- Check the functioning of horn and lights – this test is as simple as ensuring the lights aren't burnt out, and the horn operates.

- Back-up alarm (if equipped) should be checked – A backup alarm is a helpful piece of safety equipment. If equipped it must be operational, and not covered in any sound dampening material.

Week Ending: _____

The equipment operator must make this check daily at the start of the shift.

Check the appropriate box if the item is OK. If there is a problem with the item, leave the space blank and fill out the COMMENTS section below.

Visual Checks	Sun	Mon	Tues	Wed	Thur	Fri	Sat
EXCESS DIRT AND DEBRIS							
DAMAGE (Bent, dented or broken parts, paint transfer)							
LEAKS (Drive unit, brakes, hydraulics)							
TIRES & WHEELS (Drive wheels, load wheels, casters)							
FORKS (In place, properly secured, locking pins)							
CHAINS, CABLES, HOSES (In place)							
GUAGES (Operating)							
PROPANE BOTLE (relief valve, safety strap, fuel level, listen for leaks)							
ENGINE COMPARTMENT (oil, fan belt, battery, etc...)							
GUARDS (Overhead, load backrest, mast, etc.)							
SAFETY DEVICES (<u>Lights</u>, labels, seatbelt, harness, tether)							
MAST ASSEMBLY (no broken welds, no dents)							
Operational Checks	**REPORT ALL UNSAFE CONDITIONS**						
HORN (Sounds)							
STEERING (No binding, no excessive play)							
TRAVEL CONTROLS (All speed ranges, forward/reverse, etc.)							
HYDRAULIC CONTROLS (Raise & lover, tilt forward & back)							
BRAKES (Stop truck within required distance)							
PARKING BRAKE (Seat, hand, foot)							
POWER DISCONNECT (Cuts off all electric power)							
ATTACHMENTS (Function properly)							
EQUIPMENT WAS NOT USED ON THIS PARTICULAR DAY.							
OPERATOR'S INITIALS (PLEASE PRINT CLEARLY)							
Supervisor's Initials upon review:_____							

COMMENTS: (Items needing repair or adjustment)

Date:	Issue:
Resolved Date:	**Resolved By:**
COMMENTS	

CAUTION: If the equipment is found to be in need of repair or in any way unsafe, or contributes to an unsafe condition, the matter shall be reported immediately to the designated authority and the equipment shall not be operated until it has been restored to safe condition. Do not make repairs or adjustments unless specifically authorized to do so.

- Verify that all safety devices like the seat belt is in proper working condition – The seatbelt should be checked to ensure it locks on quick stops, and that it securely closes.

- Propane bottle restraints – The propane bottle should be secured in place with restraints, which must be locked in place.

- Propane level and connections – Check the level of the propane and the connection points, to ensure you have plenty of fuel for the safe operation and that it isn't leaking.

- Drive control - forward and reverse should be checked for smooth functioning.

- Hoist and lowering control should function smoothly – Check this by raising and lowering the mast, also at this point check the chain, to make sure it has adequate tension.

- Gauges: Functioning of Amp meter, engine oil pressure, Hour Meter, fuel level, temperature, and instrument monitors.

Week Ending: _____

The equipment operator must make this check daily at the start of the shift.

Check the appropriate box if the item is OK. If there is a problem with the item, leave the space blank and fill out the COMMENTS section below.

Visual Checks	Sun	Mon	Tues	Wed	Thur	Fri	Sat
EXCESS DIRT AND DEBRIS							
DAMAGE (Bent, dented or broken parts, paint transfer)							
LEAKS (Drive unit, brakes, hydraulics)							
TIRES & WHEELS (Drive wheels, load wheels, casters)							
FORKS (In place, properly secured, locking pins)							
CHAINS, CABLES, HOSES (In place)							
GUAGES (Operating)							
PROPANE BOTLE (relief valve, safety strap, fuel level, listen for leaks)							
ENGINE COMPARTMENT (oil, fan belt, battery, etc...)							
GUARDS (Overhead, load backrest, mast, etc.)							
SAFETY DEVICES (<u>Lights</u>, labels, seatbelt, harness, tether)							
MAST ASSEMBLY (no broken welds, no dents)							
Operational Checks	REPORT ALL UNSAFE CONDITIONS						
HORN (Sounds)							
STEERING (No binding, no excessive play)							
TRAVEL CONTROLS (All speed ranges, forward/reverse, etc.)							
HYDRAULIC CONTROLS (Raise & lover, tilt forward & back)							
BRAKES (Stop truck within required distance)							
PARKING BRAKE (Seat, hand, foot)							
POWER DISCONNECT (Cuts off all electric power)							
ATTACHMENTS (Function properly)							
EQUIPMENT WAS NOT USED ON THIS PARTICULAR DAY.							
OPERATOR'S INITIALS (PLEASE PRINT CLEARLY)							
Supervisor's Initials upon review:_____							

COMMENTS: (Items needing repair or adjustment)

Date:	Issue:
Resolved Date:	**Resolved By:**
COMMENTS	

CAUTION: If the equipment is found to be in need of repair or in any way unsafe, or contributes to an unsafe condition, the matter shall be reported immediately to the designated authority and the equipment shall not be operated until it has been restored to safe condition. Do not make repairs or adjustments unless specifically authorized to do so.

- Inspect tire condition:
  - Pneumatic(air filled) wheels should have pressure and now have cracks through the rubber.
  - Solid wheels should not have large cracks or gouges in them.

- Check for grease and debris in the operator compartment – this can contribute to slipping off the equipment, and cause a serious injury.

- Hood & panel latches – Does the hood and any removable side panels secure in place to no avoid opening or falling off.

- Steering should function smoothly – while testing this, ensure the steering wheel solidly reacts to movements. This should always be monitored during operation.

- Check the functioning of horn and lights – this test is as simple as ensuring the lights aren't burnt out, and the horn operates.

- Back-up alarm (if equipped) should be checked – A backup alarm is a helpful piece of safety equipment. If equipped it must be operational, and not covered in any sound dampening material.

Week Ending: _____

The equipment operator must make this check daily at the start of the shift.

Check the appropriate box if the item is OK. If there is a problem with the item, leave the space blank and fill out the COMMENTS section below.

Visual Checks	Sun	Mon	Tues	Wed	Thur	Fri	Sat
EXCESS DIRT AND DEBRIS							
DAMAGE (Bent, dented or broken parts, paint transfer)							
LEAKS (Drive unit, brakes, hydraulics)							
TIRES & WHEELS (Drive wheels, load wheels, casters)							
FORKS (In place, properly secured, locking pins)							
CHAINS, CABLES, HOSES (In place)							
GUAGES (Operating)							
PROPANE BOTLE (relief valve, safety strap, fuel level, listen for leaks)							
ENGINE COMPARTMENT (oil, fan belt, battery, etc…)							
GUARDS (Overhead, load backrest, mast, etc.)							
SAFETY DEVICES (<u>Lights</u>, labels, seatbelt, harness, tether)							
MAST ASSEMBLY (no broken welds, no dents)							
Operational Checks	**REPORT ALL UNSAFE CONDITIONS**						
HORN (Sounds)							
STEERING (No binding, no excessive play)							
TRAVEL CONTROLS (All speed ranges, forward/reverse, etc.)							
HYDRAULIC CONTROLS (Raise & lover, tilt forward & back)							
BRAKES (Stop truck within required distance)							
PARKING BRAKE (Seat, hand, foot)							
POWER DISCONNECT (Cuts off all electric power)							
ATTACHMENTS (Function properly)							
EQUIPMENT WAS NOT USED ON THIS PARTICULAR DAY.							
OPERATOR'S INITIALS (PLEASE PRINT CLEARLY)							

Supervisor's Initials upon review:_____

COMMENTS: (Items needing repair or adjustment)

Date:	Issue:
Resolved Date:	**Resolved By:**
COMMENTS	

CAUTION: If the equipment is found to be in need of repair or in any way unsafe, or contributes to an unsafe condition, the matter shall be reported immediately to the designated authority and the equipment shall not be operated until it has been restored to safe condition. Do not make repairs or adjustments unless specifically authorized to do so.

- Look out for any leaks, cracks, or visible defects in hydraulic hoses or tension in mast chains. – Checking for wet spots around hoses is how to identify hydraulic leaks, look visually around the hose connectors for cracks and bulges. Check along loop points for cracks, bulges, and frayed spots.

- Check fork condition including the top clip retaining pin and heel. – Forks should be able to be moved. Also inspect the tips of the forks, for curling or cracking.

- Check the load backrest extension and see if finger guards are attached. – Load backrest should be free from dents, deflections, or damage.

- Propane connectors for frayed tube or leaking connections. – propane connectors can become damaged over time, so visually inspect the cables and connectors for fraying on the cable and cracks or leaks on the connectors.

- Check if the **accelerator** or direction control pedal is working smoothly. – Inspect these as an operation test, by slowly moving the equipment.

- Tilt control: forward and back should be checked for smooth functioning. – Tilt the mast forward and back, quickly to verify operation is smooth and responsive.

Week Ending: _____

The equipment operator must make this check daily at the start of the shift.

Check the appropriate box if the item is OK. If there is a problem with the item, leave the space blank and fill out the COMMENTS section below.

Visual Checks	Sun	Mon	Tues	Wed	Thur	Fri	Sat
EXCESS DIRT AND DEBRIS							
DAMAGE (Bent, dented or broken parts, paint transfer)							
LEAKS (Drive unit, brakes, hydraulics)							
TIRES & WHEELS (Drive wheels, load wheels, casters)							
FORKS (In place, properly secured, locking pins)							
CHAINS, CABLES, HOSES (In place)							
GUAGES (Operating)							
PROPANE BOTLE (relief valve, safety strap, fuel level, listen for leaks)							
ENGINE COMPARTMENT (oil, fan belt, battery, etc...)							
GUARDS (Overhead, load backrest, mast, etc.)							
SAFETY DEVICES (<u>Lights</u>, labels, seatbelt, harness, tether)							
MAST ASSEMBLY (no broken welds, no dents)							
Operational Checks		**REPORT ALL UNSAFE CONDITIONS**					
HORN (Sounds)							
STEERING (No binding, no excessive play)							
TRAVEL CONTROLS (All speed ranges, forward/reverse, etc.)							
HYDRAULIC CONTROLS (Raise & lover, tilt forward & back)							
BRAKES (Stop truck within required distance)							
PARKING BRAKE (Seat, hand, foot)							
POWER DISCONNECT (Cuts off all electric power)							
ATTACHMENTS (Function properly)							
EQUIPMENT WAS NOT USED ON THIS PARTICULAR DAY.							
OPERATOR'S INITIALS (PLEASE PRINT CLEARLY)							

Supervisor's Initials upon review:_____

COMMENTS: (Items needing repair or adjustment)

Date:	Issue:
Resolved Date:	**Resolved By:**
COMMENTS	

CAUTION: If the equipment is found to be in need of repair or in any way unsafe, or contributes to an unsafe condition, the matter shall be reported immediately to the designated authority and the equipment shall not be operated until it has been restored to safe condition. Do not make repairs or adjustments unless specifically authorized to do so.

- Inspect tire condition:
  - Pneumatic(air filled) wheels should have pressure and now have cracks through the rubber.
  - Solid wheels should not have large cracks or gouges in them.

- Check for grease and debris in the operator compartment – this can contribute to slipping off the equipment, and cause a serious injury.

- Hood & panel latches – Does the hood and any removable side panels secure in place to no avoid opening or falling off.

- Steering should function smoothly – while testing this, ensure the steering wheel solidly reacts to movements. This should always be monitored during operation.

- Check the functioning of horn and lights – this test is as simple as ensuring the lights aren't burnt out, and the horn operates.

- Back-up alarm (if equipped) should be checked – A backup alarm is a helpful piece of safety equipment. If equipped it must be operational, and not covered in any sound dampening material.

Week Ending: _____

The equipment operator must make this check daily at the start of the shift.

Check the appropriate box if the item is OK. If there is a problem with the item, leave the space blank and fill out the COMMENTS section below.

Visual Checks	Sun	Mon	Tues	Wed	Thur	Fri	Sat
EXCESS DIRT AND DEBRIS							
DAMAGE (Bent, dented or broken parts, paint transfer)							
LEAKS (Drive unit, brakes, hydraulics)							
TIRES & WHEELS (Drive wheels, load wheels, casters)							
FORKS (In place, properly secured, locking pins)							
CHAINS, CABLES, HOSES (In place)							
GUAGES (Operating)							
PROPANE BOTLE (relief valve, safety strap, fuel level, listen for leaks)							
ENGINE COMPARTMENT (oil, fan belt, battery, etc…)							
GUARDS (Overhead, load backrest, mast, etc.)							
SAFETY DEVICES (<u>Lights</u>, labels, seatbelt, harness, tether)							
MAST ASSEMBLY (no broken welds, no dents)							
Operational Checks	REPORT ALL UNSAFE CONDITIONS						
HORN (Sounds)							
STEERING (No binding, no excessive play)							
TRAVEL CONTROLS (All speed ranges, forward/reverse, etc.)							
HYDRAULIC CONTROLS (Raise & lover, tilt forward & back)							
BRAKES (Stop truck within required distance)							
PARKING BRAKE (Seat, hand, foot)							
POWER DISCONNECT (Cuts off all electric power)							
ATTACHMENTS (Function properly)							
EQUIPMENT WAS NOT USED ON THIS PARTICULAR DAY.							
OPERATOR'S INITIALS (PLEASE PRINT CLEARLY)							
Supervisor's Initials upon review:_____							

COMMENTS: (Items needing repair or adjustment)

Date:	Issue:
Resolved Date:	Resolved By:
COMMENTS	

CAUTION: If the equipment is found to be in need of repair or in any way unsafe, or contributes to an unsafe condition, the matter shall be reported immediately to the designated authority and the equipment shall not be operated until it has been restored to safe condition. Do not make repairs or adjustments unless specifically authorized to do so.

- Verify that all safety devices like the seat belt is in proper working condition – The seatbelt should be checked to ensure it locks on quick stops, and that it securely closes.

- Propane bottle restraints – The propane bottle should be secured in place with restraints, which must be locked in place.

- Propane level and connections – Check the level of the propane and the connection points, to ensure you have plenty of fuel for the safe operation and that it isn't leaking.

- Drive control - forward and reverse should be checked for smooth functioning.

- Hoist and lowering control should function smoothly – Check this by raising and lowering the mast, also at this point check the chain, to make sure it has adequate tension.

- Gauges: Functioning of Amp meter, engine oil pressure, Hour Meter, fuel level, temperature, and instrument monitors.

Week Ending: _____

The equipment operator must make this check daily at the start of the shift.

Check the appropriate box if the item is OK. If there is a problem with the item, leave the space blank and fill out the COMMENTS section below.

Visual Checks	Sun	Mon	Tues	Wed	Thur	Fri	Sat
EXCESS DIRT AND DEBRIS							
DAMAGE (Bent, dented or broken parts, paint transfer)							
LEAKS (Drive unit, brakes, hydraulics)							
TIRES & WHEELS (Drive wheels, load wheels, casters)							
FORKS (In place, properly secured, locking pins)							
CHAINS, CABLES, HOSES (In place)							
GUAGES (Operating)							
PROPANE BOTLE (relief valve, safety strap, fuel level, listen for leaks)							
ENGINE COMPARTMENT (oil, fan belt, battery, etc...)							
GUARDS (Overhead, load backrest, mast, etc.)							
SAFETY DEVICES (<u>Lights</u>, labels, seatbelt, harness, tether)							
MAST ASSEMBLY (no broken welds, no dents)							
Operational Checks	REPORT ALL UNSAFE CONDITIONS						
HORN (Sounds)							
STEERING (No binding, no excessive play)							
TRAVEL CONTROLS (All speed ranges, forward/reverse, etc.)							
HYDRAULIC CONTROLS (Raise & lover, tilt forward & back)							
BRAKES (Stop truck within required distance)							
PARKING BRAKE (Seat, hand, foot)							
POWER DISCONNECT (Cuts off all electric power)							
ATTACHMENTS (Function properly)							
EQUIPMENT WAS NOT USED ON THIS PARTICULAR DAY.							
OPERATOR'S INITIALS (PLEASE PRINT CLEARLY)							
Supervisor's Initials upon review:_____							

COMMENTS: (Items needing repair or adjustment)

Date:	Issue:
Resolved Date:	**Resolved By:**
COMMENTS	

CAUTION: If the equipment is found to be in need of repair or in any way unsafe, or contributes to an unsafe condition, the matter shall be reported immediately to the designated authority and the equipment shall not be operated until it has been restored to safe condition. Do not make repairs or adjustments unless specifically authorized to do so.

- Inspect tire condition:
  - Pneumatic(air filled) wheels should have pressure and now have cracks through the rubber.
  - Solid wheels should not have large cracks or gouges in them.

- Check for grease and debris in the operator compartment – this can contribute to slipping off the equipment, and cause a serious injury.

- Hood & panel latches – Does the hood and any removable side panels secure in place to no avoid opening or falling off.

- Steering should function smoothly – while testing this, ensure the steering wheel solidly reacts to movements. This should always be monitored during operation.

- Check the functioning of horn and lights – this test is as simple as ensuring the lights aren't burnt out, and the horn operates.

- Back-up alarm (if equipped) should be checked – A backup alarm is a helpful piece of safety equipment. If equipped it must be operational, and not covered in any sound dampening material.

Week Ending: _____

The equipment operator must make this check daily at the start of the shift.

Check the appropriate box if the item is OK. If there is a problem with the item, leave the space blank and fill out the COMMENTS section below.

Visual Checks	Sun	Mon	Tues	Wed	Thur	Fri	Sat
EXCESS DIRT AND DEBRIS							
DAMAGE (Bent, dented or broken parts, paint transfer)							
LEAKS (Drive unit, brakes, hydraulics)							
TIRES & WHEELS (Drive wheels, load wheels, casters)							
FORKS (In place, properly secured, locking pins)							
CHAINS, CABLES, HOSES (In place)							
GUAGES (Operating)							
PROPANE BOTLE (relief valve, safety strap, fuel level, listen for leaks)							
ENGINE COMPARTMENT (oil, fan belt, battery, etc…)							
GUARDS (Overhead, load backrest, mast, etc.)							
SAFETY DEVICES (Lights, labels, seatbelt, harness, tether)							
MAST ASSEMBLY (no broken welds, no dents)							
Operational Checks	REPORT ALL UNSAFE CONDITIONS						
HORN (Sounds)							
STEERING (No binding, no excessive play)							
TRAVEL CONTROLS (All speed ranges, forward/reverse, etc.)							
HYDRAULIC CONTROLS (Raise & lover, tilt forward & back)							
BRAKES (Stop truck within required distance)							
PARKING BRAKE (Seat, hand, foot)							
POWER DISCONNECT (Cuts off all electric power)							
ATTACHMENTS (Function properly)							
EQUIPMENT WAS NOT USED ON THIS PARTICULAR DAY.							
OPERATOR'S INITIALS (PLEASE PRINT CLEARLY)							
Supervisor's Initials upon review:_____							

COMMENTS: (Items needing repair or adjustment)

Date:	Issue:
Resolved Date:	**Resolved By:**
COMMENTS	

CAUTION: If the equipment is found to be in need of repair or in any way unsafe, or contributes to an unsafe condition, the matter shall be reported immediately to the designated authority and the equipment shall not be operated until it has been restored to safe condition. Do not make repairs or adjustments unless specifically authorized to do so.

- Look out for any leaks, cracks, or visible defects in hydraulic hoses or tension in mast chains. – Checking for wet spots around hoses is how to identify hydraulic leaks, look visually around the hose connectors for cracks and bulges. Check along loop points for cracks, bulges, and frayed spots.

- Check fork condition including the top clip retaining pin and heel. – Forks should be able to be moved. Also inspect the tips of the forks, for curling or cracking.

- Check the load backrest extension and see if finger guards are attached. – Load backrest should be free from dents, deflections, or damage.

- Propane connectors for frayed tube or leaking connections. – propane connectors can become damaged over time, so visually inspect the cables and connectors for fraying on the cable and cracks or leaks on the connectors.

- Check if the **accelerator** or direction control pedal is working smoothly. – Inspect these as an operation test, by slowly moving the equipment.

- Tilt control: forward and back should be checked for smooth functioning. – Tilt the mast forward and back, quickly to verify operation is smooth and responsive.

Week Ending: _____
The equipment operator must make this check daily at the start of the shift.
Check the appropriate box if the item is OK. If there is a problem with the item, leave the space blank and fill out the COMMENTS section below.

Visual Checks	Sun	Mon	Tues	Wed	Thur	Fri	Sat
EXCESS DIRT AND DEBRIS							
DAMAGE (Bent, dented or broken parts, paint transfer)							
LEAKS (Drive unit, brakes, hydraulics)							
TIRES & WHEELS (Drive wheels, load wheels, casters)							
FORKS (In place, properly secured, locking pins)							
CHAINS, CABLES, HOSES (In place)							
GUAGES (Operating)							
PROPANE BOTLE (relief valve, safety strap, fuel level, listen for leaks)							
ENGINE COMPARTMENT (oil, fan belt, battery, etc...)							
GUARDS (Overhead, load backrest, mast, etc.)							
SAFETY DEVICES (<u>Lights</u>, labels, seatbelt, harness, tether)							
MAST ASSEMBLY (no broken welds, no dents)							
Operational Checks		REPORT ALL UNSAFE CONDITIONS					
HORN (Sounds)							
STEERING (No binding, no excessive play)							
TRAVEL CONTROLS (All speed ranges, forward/reverse, etc.)							
HYDRAULIC CONTROLS (Raise & lover, tilt forward & back)							
BRAKES (Stop truck within required distance)							
PARKING BRAKE (Seat, hand, foot)							
POWER DISCONNECT (Cuts off all electric power)							
ATTACHMENTS (Function properly)							
EQUIPMENT WAS NOT USED ON THIS PARTICULAR DAY.							
OPERATOR'S INITIALS (PLEASE PRINT CLEARLY)							
Supervisor's Initials upon review:_____							

COMMENTS: (Items needing repair or adjustment)

Date:	Issue:
Resolved Date:	**Resolved By:**
COMMENTS	

CAUTION: If the equipment is found to be in need of repair or in any way unsafe, or contributes to an unsafe condition, the matter shall be reported immediately to the designated authority and the equipment shall not be operated until it has been restored to safe condition. Do not make repairs or adjustments unless specifically authorized to do so.

- Inspect tire condition:
  - Pneumatic(air filled) wheels should have pressure and now have cracks through the rubber.
  - Solid wheels should not have large cracks or gouges in them.

- Check for grease and debris in the operator compartment – this can contribute to slipping off the equipment, and cause a serious injury.

- Hood & panel latches – Does the hood and any removable side panels secure in place to no avoid opening or falling off.

- Steering should function smoothly – while testing this, ensure the steering wheel solidly reacts to movements. This should always be monitored during operation.

- Check the functioning of horn and lights – this test is as simple as ensuring the lights aren't burnt out, and the horn operates.

- Back-up alarm (if equipped) should be checked – A backup alarm is a helpful piece of safety equipment. If equipped it must be operational, and not covered in any sound dampening material.

Week Ending: _____

The equipment operator must make this check daily at the start of the shift.

Check the appropriate box if the item is OK. If there is a problem with the item, leave the space blank and fill out the COMMENTS section below.

Visual Checks	Sun	Mon	Tues	Wed	Thur	Fri	Sat
EXCESS DIRT AND DEBRIS							
DAMAGE (Bent, dented or broken parts, paint transfer)							
LEAKS (Drive unit, brakes, hydraulics)							
TIRES & WHEELS (Drive wheels, load wheels, casters)							
FORKS (In place, properly secured, locking pins)							
CHAINS, CABLES, HOSES (In place)							
GUAGES (Operating)							
PROPANE BOTLE (relief valve, safety strap, fuel level, listen for leaks)							
ENGINE COMPARTMENT (oil, fan belt, battery, etc…)							
GUARDS (Overhead, load backrest, mast, etc.)							
SAFETY DEVICES (<u>Lights</u>, labels, seatbelt, harness, tether)							
MAST ASSEMBLY (no broken welds, no dents)							
Operational Checks	**REPORT ALL UNSAFE CONDITIONS**						
HORN (Sounds)							
STEERING (No binding, no excessive play)							
TRAVEL CONTROLS (All speed ranges, forward/reverse, etc.)							
HYDRAULIC CONTROLS (Raise & lover, tilt forward & back)							
BRAKES (Stop truck within required distance)							
PARKING BRAKE (Seat, hand, foot)							
POWER DISCONNECT (Cuts off all electric power)							
ATTACHMENTS (Function properly)							
EQUIPMENT WAS NOT USED ON THIS PARTICULAR DAY.							
OPERATOR'S INITIALS (PLEASE PRINT CLEARLY)							
Supervisor's Initials upon review:_____							

COMMENTS: (Items needing repair or adjustment)

Date:	Issue:
Resolved Date:	Resolved By:
COMMENTS	

CAUTION: If the equipment is found to be in need of repair or in any way unsafe, or contributes to an unsafe condition, the matter shall be reported immediately to the designated authority and the equipment shall not be operated until it has been restored to safe condition. Do not make repairs or adjustments unless specifically authorized to do so.

- Verify that all safety devices like the seat belt is in proper working condition – The seatbelt should be checked to ensure it locks on quick stops, and that it securely closes.

- Propane bottle restraints – The propane bottle should be secured in place with restraints, which must be locked in place.

- Propane level and connections – Check the level of the propane and the connection points, to ensure you have plenty of fuel for the safe operation and that it isn't leaking.

- Drive control - forward and reverse should be checked for smooth functioning.

- Hoist and lowering control should function smoothly – Check this by raising and lowering the mast, also at this point check the chain, to make sure it has adequate tension.

- Gauges: Functioning of Amp meter, engine oil pressure, Hour Meter, fuel level, temperature, and instrument monitors.

Week Ending: _____

The equipment operator must make this check daily at the start of the shift.

Check the appropriate box if the item is OK. If there is a problem with the item, leave the space blank and fill out the COMMENTS section below.

Visual Checks	Sun	Mon	Tues	Wed	Thur	Fri	Sat
EXCESS DIRT AND DEBRIS							
DAMAGE (Bent, dented or broken parts, paint transfer)							
LEAKS (Drive unit, brakes, hydraulics)							
TIRES & WHEELS (Drive wheels, load wheels, casters)							
FORKS (In place, properly secured, locking pins)							
CHAINS, CABLES, HOSES (In place)							
GUAGES (Operating)							
PROPANE BOTLE (relief valve, safety strap, fuel level, listen for leaks)							
ENGINE COMPARTMENT (oil, fan belt, battery, etc...)							
GUARDS (Overhead, load backrest, mast, etc.)							
SAFETY DEVICES (<u>Lights</u>, labels, seatbelt, harness, tether)							
MAST ASSEMBLY (no broken welds, no dents)							
Operational Checks	REPORT ALL UNSAFE CONDITIONS						
HORN (Sounds)							
STEERING (No binding, no excessive play)							
TRAVEL CONTROLS (All speed ranges, forward/reverse, etc.)							
HYDRAULIC CONTROLS (Raise & lover, tilt forward & back)							
BRAKES (Stop truck within required distance)							
PARKING BRAKE (Seat, hand, foot)							
POWER DISCONNECT (Cuts off all electric power)							
ATTACHMENTS (Function properly)							
EQUIPMENT WAS NOT USED ON THIS PARTICULAR DAY.							
OPERATOR'S INITIALS (PLEASE PRINT CLEARLY)							

Supervisor's Initials upon review:_____

COMMENTS: (Items needing repair or adjustment)

Date:	Issue:
Resolved Date:	**Resolved By:**
COMMENTS	

CAUTION: If the equipment is found to be in need of repair or in any way unsafe, or contributes to an unsafe condition, the matter shall be reported immediately to the designated authority and the equipment shall not be operated until it has been restored to safe condition. Do not make repairs or adjustments unless specifically authorized to do so.

- Inspect tire condition:
    - Pneumatic(air filled) wheels should have pressure and now have cracks through the rubber.
    - Solid wheels should not have large cracks or gouges in them.

- Check for grease and debris in the operator compartment – this can contribute to slipping off the equipment, and cause a serious injury.

- Hood & panel latches – Does the hood and any removable side panels secure in place to no avoid opening or falling off.

- Steering should function smoothly – while testing this, ensure the steering wheel solidly reacts to movements. This should always be monitored during operation.

- Check the functioning of horn and lights – this test is as simple as ensuring the lights aren't burnt out, and the horn operates.

- Back-up alarm (if equipped) should be checked – A backup alarm is a helpful piece of safety equipment. If equipped it must be operational, and not covered in any sound dampening material.

Week Ending: _____

The equipment operator must make this check daily at the start of the shift.

Check the appropriate box if the item is OK. If there is a problem with the item, leave the space blank and fill out the COMMENTS section below.

Visual Checks	Sun	Mon	Tues	Wed	Thur	Fri	Sat
EXCESS DIRT AND DEBRIS							
DAMAGE (Bent, dented or broken parts, paint transfer)							
LEAKS (Drive unit, brakes, hydraulics)							
TIRES & WHEELS (Drive wheels, load wheels, casters)							
FORKS (In place, properly secured, locking pins)							
CHAINS, CABLES, HOSES (In place)							
GUAGES (Operating)							
PROPANE BOTLE (relief valve, safety strap, fuel level, listen for leaks)							
ENGINE COMPARTMENT (oil, fan belt, battery, etc...)							
GUARDS (Overhead, load backrest, mast, etc.)							
SAFETY DEVICES (<u>Lights</u>, labels, seatbelt, harness, tether)							
MAST ASSEMBLY (no broken welds, no dents)							
Operational Checks	**REPORT ALL UNSAFE CONDITIONS**						
HORN (Sounds)							
STEERING (No binding, no excessive play)							
TRAVEL CONTROLS (All speed ranges, forward/reverse, etc.)							
HYDRAULIC CONTROLS (Raise & lover, tilt forward & back)							
BRAKES (Stop truck within required distance)							
PARKING BRAKE (Seat, hand, foot)							
POWER DISCONNECT (Cuts off all electric power)							
ATTACHMENTS (Function properly)							
EQUIPMENT WAS NOT USED ON THIS PARTICULAR DAY.							
OPERATOR'S INITIALS (PLEASE PRINT CLEARLY)							

Supervisor's Initials upon review:_____

COMMENTS: (Items needing repair or adjustment)

Date:	Issue:
Resolved Date:	Resolved By:
COMMENTS	

CAUTION: If the equipment is found to be in need of repair or in any way unsafe, or contributes to an unsafe condition, the matter shall be reported immediately to the designated authority and the equipment shall not be operated until it has been restored to safe condition. Do not make repairs or adjustments unless specifically authorized to do so.

- Look out for any leaks, cracks, or visible defects in hydraulic hoses or tension in mast chains. – Checking for wet spots around hoses is how to identify hydraulic leaks, look visually around the hose connectors for cracks and bulges. Check along loop points for cracks, bulges, and frayed spots.

- Check fork condition including the top clip retaining pin and heel. – Forks should be able to be moved. Also inspect the tips of the forks, for curling or cracking.

- Check the load backrest extension and see if finger guards are attached. – Load backrest should be free from dents, deflections, or damage.

- Propane connectors for frayed tube or leaking connections. – propane connectors can become damaged over time, so visually inspect the cables and connectors for fraying on the cable and cracks or leaks on the connectors.

- Check if the **accelerator** or direction control pedal is working smoothly. – Inspect these as an operation test, by slowly moving the equipment.

- Tilt control: forward and back should be checked for smooth functioning. – Tilt the mast forward and back, quickly to verify operation is smooth and responsive.

Week Ending: _____

The equipment operator must make this check daily at the start of the shift.

Check the appropriate box if the item is OK. If there is a problem with the item, leave the space blank and fill out the COMMENTS section below.

Visual Checks	Sun	Mon	Tues	Wed	Thur	Fri	Sat
EXCESS DIRT AND DEBRIS							
DAMAGE (Bent, dented or broken parts, paint transfer)							
LEAKS (Drive unit, brakes, hydraulics)							
TIRES & WHEELS (Drive wheels, load wheels, casters)							
FORKS (In place, properly secured, locking pins)							
CHAINS, CABLES, HOSES (In place)							
GUAGES (Operating)							
PROPANE BOTLE (relief valve, safety strap, fuel level, listen for leaks)							
ENGINE COMPARTMENT (oil, fan belt, battery, etc...)							
GUARDS (Overhead, load backrest, mast, etc.)							
SAFETY DEVICES (<u>Lights</u>, labels, seatbelt, harness, tether)							
MAST ASSEMBLY (no broken welds, no dents)							
Operational Checks		**REPORT ALL UNSAFE CONDITIONS**					
HORN (Sounds)							
STEERING (No binding, no excessive play)							
TRAVEL CONTROLS (All speed ranges, forward/reverse, etc.)							
HYDRAULIC CONTROLS (Raise & lover, tilt forward & back)							
BRAKES (Stop truck within required distance)							
PARKING BRAKE (Seat, hand, foot)							
POWER DISCONNECT (Cuts off all electric power)							
ATTACHMENTS (Function properly)							
EQUIPMENT WAS NOT USED ON THIS PARTICULAR DAY.							
OPERATOR'S INITIALS (PLEASE PRINT CLEARLY)							
Supervisor's Initials upon review:_____							

COMMENTS: (Items needing repair or adjustment)

Date:	Issue:
Resolved Date:	**Resolved By:**
COMMENTS	

CAUTION: If the equipment is found to be in need of repair or in any way unsafe, or contributes to an unsafe condition, the matter shall be reported immediately to the designated authority and the equipment shall not be operated until it has been restored to safe condition. Do not make repairs or adjustments unless specifically authorized to do so.

- Inspect tire condition:
  - Pneumatic(air filled) wheels should have pressure and now have cracks through the rubber.
  - Solid wheels should not have large cracks or gouges in them.

- Check for grease and debris in the operator compartment – this can contribute to slipping off the equipment, and cause a serious injury.

- Hood & panel latches – Does the hood and any removable side panels secure in place to no avoid opening or falling off.

- Steering should function smoothly – while testing this, ensure the steering wheel solidly reacts to movements. This should always be monitored during operation.

- Check the functioning of horn and lights – this test is as simple as ensuring the lights aren't burnt out, and the horn operates.

- Back-up alarm (if equipped) should be checked – A backup alarm is a helpful piece of safety equipment. If equipped it must be operational, and not covered in any sound dampening material.

Week Ending: _____

The equipment operator must make this check daily at the start of the shift.

Check the appropriate box if the item is OK. If there is a problem with the item, leave the space blank and fill out the COMMENTS section below.

Visual Checks	Sun	Mon	Tues	Wed	Thur	Fri	Sat
EXCESS DIRT AND DEBRIS							
DAMAGE (Bent, dented or broken parts, paint transfer)							
LEAKS (Drive unit, brakes, hydraulics)							
TIRES & WHEELS (Drive wheels, load wheels, casters)							
FORKS (In place, properly secured, locking pins)							
CHAINS, CABLES, HOSES (In place)							
GUAGES (Operating)							
PROPANE BOTLE (relief valve, safety strap, fuel level, listen for leaks)							
ENGINE COMPARTMENT (oil, fan belt, battery, etc…)							
GUARDS (Overhead, load backrest, mast, etc.)							
SAFETY DEVICES (Lights, labels, seatbelt, harness, tether)							
MAST ASSEMBLY (no broken welds, no dents)							
Operational Checks	**REPORT ALL UNSAFE CONDITIONS**						
HORN (Sounds)							
STEERING (No binding, no excessive play)							
TRAVEL CONTROLS (All speed ranges, forward/reverse, etc.)							
HYDRAULIC CONTROLS (Raise & lover, tilt forward & back)							
BRAKES (Stop truck within required distance)							
PARKING BRAKE (Seat, hand, foot)							
POWER DISCONNECT (Cuts off all electric power)							
ATTACHMENTS (Function properly)							
EQUIPMENT WAS NOT USED ON THIS PARTICULAR DAY.							
OPERATOR'S INITIALS (PLEASE PRINT CLEARLY)							
Supervisor's Initials upon review:_____							

COMMENTS: (Items needing repair or adjustment)

Date:	Issue:
Resolved Date:	**Resolved By:**
COMMENTS	

CAUTION: If the equipment is found to be in need of repair or in any way unsafe, or contributes to an unsafe condition, the matter shall be reported immediately to the designated authority and the equipment shall not be operated until it has been restored to safe condition. Do not make repairs or adjustments unless specifically authorized to do so.

- Verify that all safety devices like the seat belt is in proper working condition – The seatbelt should be checked to ensure it locks on quick stops, and that it securely closes.

- Propane bottle restraints – The propane bottle should be secured in place with restraints, which must be locked in place.

- Propane level and connections – Check the level of the propane and the connection points, to ensure you have plenty of fuel for the safe operation and that it isn't leaking.

- Drive control - forward and reverse should be checked for smooth functioning.

- Hoist and lowering control should function smoothly – Check this by raising and lowering the mast, also at this point check the chain, to make sure it has adequate tension.

- Gauges: Functioning of Amp meter, engine oil pressure, Hour Meter, fuel level, temperature, and instrument monitors.

Week Ending: _____

The equipment operator must make this check daily at the start of the shift.

Check the appropriate box if the item is OK. If there is a problem with the item, leave the space blank and fill out the COMMENTS section below.

Visual Checks	Sun	Mon	Tues	Wed	Thur	Fri	Sat
EXCESS DIRT AND DEBRIS							
DAMAGE (Bent, dented or broken parts, paint transfer)							
LEAKS (Drive unit, brakes, hydraulics)							
TIRES & WHEELS (Drive wheels, load wheels, casters)							
FORKS (In place, properly secured, locking pins)							
CHAINS, CABLES, HOSES (In place)							
GUAGES (Operating)							
PROPANE BOTLE (relief valve, safety strap, fuel level, listen for leaks)							
ENGINE COMPARTMENT (oil, fan belt, battery, etc...)							
GUARDS (Overhead, load backrest, mast, etc.)							
SAFETY DEVICES (<u>Lights</u>, labels, seatbelt, harness, tether)							
MAST ASSEMBLY (no broken welds, no dents)							
Operational Checks	**REPORT ALL UNSAFE CONDITIONS**						
HORN (Sounds)							
STEERING (No binding, no excessive play)							
TRAVEL CONTROLS (All speed ranges, forward/reverse, etc.)							
HYDRAULIC CONTROLS (Raise & lover, tilt forward & back)							
BRAKES (Stop truck within required distance)							
PARKING BRAKE (Seat, hand, foot)							
POWER DISCONNECT (Cuts off all electric power)							
ATTACHMENTS (Function properly)							
EQUIPMENT WAS NOT USED ON THIS PARTICULAR DAY.							
OPERATOR'S INITIALS (PLEASE PRINT CLEARLY)							

Supervisor's Initials upon review:_____

COMMENTS: (Items needing repair or adjustment)

Date:	Issue:
Resolved Date:	**Resolved By:**
COMMENTS	

CAUTION: If the equipment is found to be in need of repair or in any way unsafe, or contributes to an unsafe condition, the matter shall be reported immediately to the designated authority and the equipment shall not be operated until it has been restored to safe condition. Do not make repairs or adjustments unless specifically authorized to do so.

- Inspect tire condition:
  - Pneumatic(air filled) wheels should have pressure and now have cracks through the rubber.
  - Solid wheels should not have large cracks or gouges in them.

- Check for grease and debris in the operator compartment – this can contribute to slipping off the equipment, and cause a serious injury.

- Hood & panel latches – Does the hood and any removable side panels secure in place to no avoid opening or falling off.

- Steering should function smoothly – while testing this, ensure the steering wheel solidly reacts to movements. This should always be monitored during operation.

- Check the functioning of horn and lights – this test is as simple as ensuring the lights aren't burnt out, and the horn operates.

- Back-up alarm (if equipped) should be checked – A backup alarm is a helpful piece of safety equipment. If equipped it must be operational, and not covered in any sound dampening material.

Week Ending: _____

The equipment operator must make this check daily at the start of the shift.

Check the appropriate box if the item is OK. If there is a problem with the item, leave the space blank and fill out the COMMENTS section below.

Visual Checks	Sun	Mon	Tues	Wed	Thur	Fri	Sat
EXCESS DIRT AND DEBRIS							
DAMAGE (Bent, dented or broken parts, paint transfer)							
LEAKS (Drive unit, brakes, hydraulics)							
TIRES & WHEELS (Drive wheels, load wheels, casters)							
FORKS (In place, properly secured, locking pins)							
CHAINS, CABLES, HOSES (In place)							
GUAGES (Operating)							
PROPANE BOTLE (relief valve, safety strap, fuel level, listen for leaks)							
ENGINE COMPARTMENT (oil, fan belt, battery, etc...)							
GUARDS (Overhead, load backrest, mast, etc.)							
SAFETY DEVICES (<u>Lights</u>, labels, seatbelt, harness, tether)							
MAST ASSEMBLY (no broken welds, no dents)							
Operational Checks	REPORT ALL UNSAFE CONDITIONS						
HORN (Sounds)							
STEERING (No binding, no excessive play)							
TRAVEL CONTROLS (All speed ranges, forward/reverse, etc.)							
HYDRAULIC CONTROLS (Raise & lover, tilt forward & back)							
BRAKES (Stop truck within required distance)							
PARKING BRAKE (Seat, hand, foot)							
POWER DISCONNECT (Cuts off all electric power)							
ATTACHMENTS (Function properly)							
EQUIPMENT WAS NOT USED ON THIS PARTICULAR DAY.							
OPERATOR'S INITIALS (PLEASE PRINT CLEARLY)							

Supervisor's Initials upon review:_____

COMMENTS: (Items needing repair or adjustment)

Date:	Issue:
Resolved Date:	**Resolved By:**
COMMENTS	

CAUTION: If the equipment is found to be in need of repair or in any way unsafe, or contributes to an unsafe condition, the matter shall be reported immediately to the designated authority and the equipment shall not be operated until it has been restored to safe condition. Do not make repairs or adjustments unless specifically authorized to do so.

- Look out for any leaks, cracks, or visible defects in hydraulic hoses or tension in mast chains. – Checking for wet spots around hoses is how to identify hydraulic leaks, look visually around the hose connectors for cracks and bulges. Check along loop points for cracks, bulges, and frayed spots.

- Check fork condition including the top clip retaining pin and heel. – Forks should be able to be moved. Also inspect the tips of the forks, for curling or cracking.

- Check the load backrest extension and see if finger guards are attached. – Load backrest should be free from dents, deflections, or damage.

- Propane connectors for frayed tube or leaking connections. – propane connectors can become damaged over time, so visually inspect the cables and connectors for fraying on the cable and cracks or leaks on the connectors.

- Check if the **accelerator** or direction control pedal is working smoothly. – Inspect these as an operation test, by slowly moving the equipment.

- Tilt control: forward and back should be checked for smooth functioning. – Tilt the mast forward and back, quickly to verify operation is smooth and responsive.

Week Ending: _____

The equipment operator must make this check daily at the start of the shift.

Check the appropriate box if the item is OK. If there is a problem with the item, leave the space blank and fill out the COMMENTS section below.

Visual Checks	Sun	Mon	Tues	Wed	Thur	Fri	Sat
EXCESS DIRT AND DEBRIS							
DAMAGE (Bent, dented or broken parts, paint transfer)							
LEAKS (Drive unit, brakes, hydraulics)							
TIRES & WHEELS (Drive wheels, load wheels, casters)							
FORKS (In place, properly secured, locking pins)							
CHAINS, CABLES, HOSES (In place)							
GUAGES (Operating)							
PROPANE BOTLE (relief valve, safety strap, fuel level, listen for leaks)							
ENGINE COMPARTMENT (oil, fan belt, battery, etc...)							
GUARDS (Overhead, load backrest, mast, etc.)							
SAFETY DEVICES (<u>Lights</u>, labels, seatbelt, harness, tether)							
MAST ASSEMBLY (no broken welds, no dents)							
Operational Checks	REPORT ALL UNSAFE CONDITIONS						
HORN (Sounds)							
STEERING (No binding, no excessive play)							
TRAVEL CONTROLS (All speed ranges, forward/reverse, etc.)							
HYDRAULIC CONTROLS (Raise & lover, tilt forward & back)							
BRAKES (Stop truck within required distance)							
PARKING BRAKE (Seat, hand, foot)							
POWER DISCONNECT (Cuts off all electric power)							
ATTACHMENTS (Function properly)							
EQUIPMENT WAS NOT USED ON THIS PARTICULAR DAY.							
OPERATOR'S INITIALS (PLEASE PRINT CLEARLY)							
Supervisor's Initials upon review:_____							

COMMENTS: (Items needing repair or adjustment)

Date:	Issue:
Resolved Date:	**Resolved By:**
COMMENTS	

CAUTION: If the equipment is found to be in need of repair or in any way unsafe, or contributes to an unsafe condition, the matter shall be reported immediately to the designated authority and the equipment shall not be operated until it has been restored to safe condition. Do not make repairs or adjustments unless specifically authorized to do so.

- Inspect tire condition:
    - Pneumatic(air filled) wheels should have pressure and now have cracks through the rubber.
    - Solid wheels should not have large cracks or gouges in them.

- Check for grease and debris in the operator compartment – this can contribute to slipping off the equipment, and cause a serious injury.

- Hood & panel latches – Does the hood and any removable side panels secure in place to no avoid opening or falling off.

- Steering should function smoothly – while testing this, ensure the steering wheel solidly reacts to movements. This should always be monitored during operation.

- Check the functioning of horn and lights – this test is as simple as ensuring the lights aren't burnt out, and the horn operates.

- Back-up alarm (if equipped) should be checked – A backup alarm is a helpful piece of safety equipment. If equipped it must be operational, and not covered in any sound dampening material.

Week Ending: _____							
The equipment operator must make this check daily at the start of the shift.							
Check the appropriate box if the item is OK. If there is a problem with the item, leave the space blank and fill out the COMMENTS section below.							

Visual Checks	Sun	Mon	Tues	Wed	Thur	Fri	Sat
EXCESS DIRT AND DEBRIS							
DAMAGE (Bent, dented or broken parts, paint transfer)							
LEAKS (Drive unit, brakes, hydraulics)							
TIRES & WHEELS (Drive wheels, load wheels, casters)							
FORKS (In place, properly secured, locking pins)							
CHAINS, CABLES, HOSES (In place)							
GUAGES (Operating)							
PROPANE BOTLE (relief valve, safety strap, fuel level, listen for leaks)							
ENGINE COMPARTMENT (oil, fan belt, battery, etc...)							
GUARDS (Overhead, load backrest, mast, etc.)							
SAFETY DEVICES (<u>Lights</u>, labels, seatbelt, harness, tether)							
MAST ASSEMBLY (no broken welds, no dents)							
Operational Checks	**REPORT ALL UNSAFE CONDITIONS**						
HORN (Sounds)							
STEERING (No binding, no excessive play)							
TRAVEL CONTROLS (All speed ranges, forward/reverse, etc.)							
HYDRAULIC CONTROLS (Raise & lover, tilt forward & back)							
BRAKES (Stop truck within required distance)							
PARKING BRAKE (Seat, hand, foot)							
POWER DISCONNECT (Cuts off all electric power)							
ATTACHMENTS (Function properly)							
EQUIPMENT WAS NOT USED ON THIS PARTICULAR DAY.							
OPERATOR'S INITIALS (PLEASE PRINT CLEARLY)							
Supervisor's Initials upon review:_____							

COMMENTS: (Items needing repair or adjustment)

Date:	Issue:
Resolved Date:	**Resolved By:**
COMMENTS	

CAUTION: If the equipment is found to be in need of repair or in any way unsafe, or contributes to an unsafe condition, the matter shall be reported immediately to the designated authority and the equipment shall not be operated until it has been restored to safe condition. Do not make repairs or adjustments unless specifically authorized to do so.

- Verify that all safety devices like the seat belt is in proper working condition – The seatbelt should be checked to ensure it locks on quick stops, and that it securely closes.

- Propane bottle restraints – The propane bottle should be secured in place with restraints, which must be locked in place.

- Propane level and connections – Check the level of the propane and the connection points, to ensure you have plenty of fuel for the safe operation and that it isn't leaking.

- Drive control - forward and reverse should be checked for smooth functioning.

- Hoist and lowering control should function smoothly – Check this by raising and lowering the mast, also at this point check the chain, to make sure it has adequate tension.

- Gauges: Functioning of Amp meter, engine oil pressure, Hour Meter, fuel level, temperature, and instrument monitors.

Week Ending: _____

The equipment operator must make this check daily at the start of the shift.

Check the appropriate box if the item is OK. If there is a problem with the item, leave the space blank and fill out the COMMENTS section below.

Visual Checks	Sun	Mon	Tues	Wed	Thur	Fri	Sat
EXCESS DIRT AND DEBRIS							
DAMAGE (Bent, dented or broken parts, paint transfer)							
LEAKS (Drive unit, brakes, hydraulics)							
TIRES & WHEELS (Drive wheels, load wheels, casters)							
FORKS (In place, properly secured, locking pins)							
CHAINS, CABLES, HOSES (In place)							
GUAGES (Operating)							
PROPANE BOTLE (relief valve, safety strap, fuel level, listen for leaks)							
ENGINE COMPARTMENT (oil, fan belt, battery, etc…)							
GUARDS (Overhead, load backrest, mast, etc.)							
SAFETY DEVICES (<u>Lights</u>, labels, seatbelt, harness, tether)							
MAST ASSEMBLY (no broken welds, no dents)							
Operational Checks	REPORT ALL UNSAFE CONDITIONS						
HORN (Sounds)							
STEERING (No binding, no excessive play)							
TRAVEL CONTROLS (All speed ranges, forward/reverse, etc.)							
HYDRAULIC CONTROLS (Raise & lover, tilt forward & back)							
BRAKES (Stop truck within required distance)							
PARKING BRAKE (Seat, hand, foot)							
POWER DISCONNECT (Cuts off all electric power)							
ATTACHMENTS (Function properly)							
EQUIPMENT WAS NOT USED ON THIS PARTICULAR DAY.							
OPERATOR'S INITIALS (PLEASE PRINT CLEARLY)							

Supervisor's Initials upon review:_____

COMMENTS: (Items needing repair or adjustment)

Date:	Issue:
Resolved Date:	**Resolved By:**
COMMENTS	

CAUTION: If the equipment is found to be in need of repair or in any way unsafe, or contributes to an unsafe condition, the matter shall be reported immediately to the designated authority and the equipment shall not be operated until it has been restored to safe condition. Do not make repairs or adjustments unless specifically authorized to do so.

- Inspect tire condition:
  - Pneumatic(air filled) wheels should have pressure and now have cracks through the rubber.
  - Solid wheels should not have large cracks or gouges in them.

- Check for grease and debris in the operator compartment – this can contribute to slipping off the equipment, and cause a serious injury.

- Hood & panel latches – Does the hood and any removable side panels secure in place to no avoid opening or falling off.

- Steering should function smoothly – while testing this, ensure the steering wheel solidly reacts to movements. This should always be monitored during operation.

- Check the functioning of horn and lights – this test is as simple as ensuring the lights aren't burnt out, and the horn operates.

- Back-up alarm (if equipped) should be checked – A backup alarm is a helpful piece of safety equipment. If equipped it must be operational, and not covered in any sound dampening material.

Week Ending: _____

The equipment operator must make this check daily at the start of the shift.

Check the appropriate box if the item is OK. If there is a problem with the item, leave the space blank and fill out the COMMENTS section below.

Visual Checks	Sun	Mon	Tues	Wed	Thur	Fri	Sat
EXCESS DIRT AND DEBRIS							
DAMAGE (Bent, dented or broken parts, paint transfer)							
LEAKS (Drive unit, brakes, hydraulics)							
TIRES & WHEELS (Drive wheels, load wheels, casters)							
FORKS (In place, properly secured, locking pins)							
CHAINS, CABLES, HOSES (In place)							
GUAGES (Operating)							
PROPANE BOTLE (relief valve, safety strap, fuel level, listen for leaks)							
ENGINE COMPARTMENT (oil, fan belt, battery, etc…)							
GUARDS (Overhead, load backrest, mast, etc.)							
SAFETY DEVICES (Lights, labels, seatbelt, harness, tether)							
MAST ASSEMBLY (no broken welds, no dents)							
Operational Checks	REPORT ALL UNSAFE CONDITIONS						
HORN (Sounds)							
STEERING (No binding, no excessive play)							
TRAVEL CONTROLS (All speed ranges, forward/reverse, etc.)							
HYDRAULIC CONTROLS (Raise & lover, tilt forward & back)							
BRAKES (Stop truck within required distance)							
PARKING BRAKE (Seat, hand, foot)							
POWER DISCONNECT (Cuts off all electric power)							
ATTACHMENTS (Function properly)							
EQUIPMENT WAS NOT USED ON THIS PARTICULAR DAY.							
OPERATOR'S INITIALS (PLEASE PRINT CLEARLY)							
Supervisor's Initials upon review:_____							

COMMENTS: (Items needing repair or adjustment)

Date:	Issue:
Resolved Date:	**Resolved By:**
COMMENTS	

CAUTION: If the equipment is found to be in need of repair or in any way unsafe, or contributes to an unsafe condition, the matter shall be reported immediately to the designated authority and the equipment shall not be operated until it has been restored to safe condition. Do not make repairs or adjustments unless specifically authorized to do so.

- Look out for any leaks, cracks, or visible defects in hydraulic hoses or tension in mast chains. – Checking for wet spots around hoses is how to identify hydraulic leaks, look visually around the hose connectors for cracks and bulges. Check along loop points for cracks, bulges, and frayed spots.

- Check fork condition including the top clip retaining pin and heel. – Forks should be able to be moved. Also inspect the tips of the forks, for curling or cracking.

- Check the load backrest extension and see if finger guards are attached. – Load backrest should be free from dents, deflections, or damage.

- Propane connectors for frayed tube or leaking connections. – propane connectors can become damaged over time, so visually inspect the cables and connectors for fraying on the cable and cracks or leaks on the connectors.

- Check if the **accelerator** or direction control pedal is working smoothly. – Inspect these as an operation test, by slowly moving the equipment.

- Tilt control: forward and back should be checked for smooth functioning. – Tilt the mast forward and back, quickly to verify operation is smooth and responsive.

Week Ending: _____

The equipment operator must make this check daily at the start of the shift.

Check the appropriate box if the item is OK. If there is a problem with the item, leave the space blank and fill out the COMMENTS section below.

Visual Checks	Sun	Mon	Tues	Wed	Thur	Fri	Sat
EXCESS DIRT AND DEBRIS							
DAMAGE (Bent, dented or broken parts, paint transfer)							
LEAKS (Drive unit, brakes, hydraulics)							
TIRES & WHEELS (Drive wheels, load wheels, casters)							
FORKS (In place, properly secured, locking pins)							
CHAINS, CABLES, HOSES (In place)							
GUAGES (Operating)							
PROPANE BOTLE (relief valve, safety strap, fuel level, listen for leaks)							
ENGINE COMPARTMENT (oil, fan belt, battery, etc…)							
GUARDS (Overhead, load backrest, mast, etc.)							
SAFETY DEVICES (<u>Lights</u>, labels, seatbelt, harness, tether)							
MAST ASSEMBLY (no broken welds, no dents)							
Operational Checks	REPORT ALL UNSAFE CONDITIONS						
HORN (Sounds)							
STEERING (No binding, no excessive play)							
TRAVEL CONTROLS (All speed ranges, forward/reverse, etc.)							
HYDRAULIC CONTROLS (Raise & lover, tilt forward & back)							
BRAKES (Stop truck within required distance)							
PARKING BRAKE (Seat, hand, foot)							
POWER DISCONNECT (Cuts off all electric power)							
ATTACHMENTS (Function properly)							
EQUIPMENT WAS NOT USED ON THIS PARTICULAR DAY.							
OPERATOR'S INITIALS (PLEASE PRINT CLEARLY)							
Supervisor's Initials upon review:_____							

COMMENTS: (Items needing repair or adjustment)

Date:	Issue:
Resolved Date:	**Resolved By:**
COMMENTS	

CAUTION: If the equipment is found to be in need of repair or in any way unsafe, or contributes to an unsafe condition, the matter shall be reported immediately to the designated authority and the equipment shall not be operated until it has been restored to safe condition. Do not make repairs or adjustments unless specifically authorized to do so.

- Inspect tire condition:
  - Pneumatic(air filled) wheels should have pressure and now have cracks through the rubber.
  - Solid wheels should not have large cracks or gouges in them.

- Check for grease and debris in the operator compartment – this can contribute to slipping off the equipment, and cause a serious injury.

- Hood & panel latches – Does the hood and any removable side panels secure in place to no avoid opening or falling off.

- Steering should function smoothly – while testing this, ensure the steering wheel solidly reacts to movements. This should always be monitored during operation.

- Check the functioning of horn and lights – this test is as simple as ensuring the lights aren't burnt out, and the horn operates.

- Back-up alarm (if equipped) should be checked – A backup alarm is a helpful piece of safety equipment. If equipped it must be operational, and not covered in any sound dampening material.

Week Ending: _____

The equipment operator must make this check daily at the start of the shift.

Check the appropriate box if the item is OK. If there is a problem with the item, leave the space blank and fill out the COMMENTS section below.

Visual Checks	Sun	Mon	Tues	Wed	Thur	Fri	Sat
EXCESS DIRT AND DEBRIS							
DAMAGE (Bent, dented or broken parts, paint transfer)							
LEAKS (Drive unit, brakes, hydraulics)							
TIRES & WHEELS (Drive wheels, load wheels, casters)							
FORKS (In place, properly secured, locking pins)							
CHAINS, CABLES, HOSES (In place)							
GUAGES (Operating)							
PROPANE BOTLE (relief valve, safety strap, fuel level, listen for leaks)							
ENGINE COMPARTMENT (oil, fan belt, battery, etc...)							
GUARDS (Overhead, load backrest, mast, etc.)							
SAFETY DEVICES (<u>Lights</u>, labels, seatbelt, harness, tether)							
MAST ASSEMBLY (no broken welds, no dents)							
Operational Checks	**REPORT ALL UNSAFE CONDITIONS**						
HORN (Sounds)							
STEERING (No binding, no excessive play)							
TRAVEL CONTROLS (All speed ranges, forward/reverse, etc.)							
HYDRAULIC CONTROLS (Raise & lover, tilt forward & back)							
BRAKES (Stop truck within required distance)							
PARKING BRAKE (Seat, hand, foot)							
POWER DISCONNECT (Cuts off all electric power)							
ATTACHMENTS (Function properly)							
EQUIPMENT WAS NOT USED ON THIS PARTICULAR DAY.							
OPERATOR'S INITIALS (PLEASE PRINT CLEARLY)							
Supervisor's Initials upon review:_____							

COMMENTS: (Items needing repair or adjustment)

Date:	Issue:
Resolved Date:	**Resolved By:**
COMMENTS	

CAUTION: If the equipment is found to be in need of repair or in any way unsafe, or contributes to an unsafe condition, the matter shall be reported immediately to the designated authority and the equipment shall not be operated until it has been restored to safe condition. Do not make repairs or adjustments unless specifically authorized to do so.

- Verify that all safety devices like the seat belt is in proper working condition – The seatbelt should be checked to ensure it locks on quick stops, and that it securely closes.

- Propane bottle restraints – The propane bottle should be secured in place with restraints, which must be locked in place.

- Propane level and connections – Check the level of the propane and the connection points, to ensure you have plenty of fuel for the safe operation and that it isn't leaking.

- Drive control - forward and reverse should be checked for smooth functioning.

- Hoist and lowering control should function smoothly – Check this by raising and lowering the mast, also at this point check the chain, to make sure it has adequate tension.

- Gauges: Functioning of Amp meter, engine oil pressure, Hour Meter, fuel level, temperature, and instrument monitors.

Week Ending: _____

The equipment operator must make this check daily at the start of the shift.

Check the appropriate box if the item is OK. If there is a problem with the item, leave the space blank and fill out the COMMENTS section below.

Visual Checks	Sun	Mon	Tues	Wed	Thur	Fri	Sat
EXCESS DIRT AND DEBRIS							
DAMAGE (Bent, dented or broken parts, paint transfer)							
LEAKS (Drive unit, brakes, hydraulics)							
TIRES & WHEELS (Drive wheels, load wheels, casters)							
FORKS (In place, properly secured, locking pins)							
CHAINS, CABLES, HOSES (In place)							
GUAGES (Operating)							
PROPANE BOTLE (relief valve, safety strap, fuel level, listen for leaks)							
ENGINE COMPARTMENT (oil, fan belt, battery, etc…)							
GUARDS (Overhead, load backrest, mast, etc.)							
SAFETY DEVICES (Lights, labels, seatbelt, harness, tether)							
MAST ASSEMBLY (no broken welds, no dents)							
Operational Checks	REPORT ALL UNSAFE CONDITIONS						
HORN (Sounds)							
STEERING (No binding, no excessive play)							
TRAVEL CONTROLS (All speed ranges, forward/reverse, etc.)							
HYDRAULIC CONTROLS (Raise & lover, tilt forward & back)							
BRAKES (Stop truck within required distance)							
PARKING BRAKE (Seat, hand, foot)							
POWER DISCONNECT (Cuts off all electric power)							
ATTACHMENTS (Function properly)							
EQUIPMENT WAS NOT USED ON THIS PARTICULAR DAY.							
OPERATOR'S INITIALS (PLEASE PRINT CLEARLY)							
Supervisor's Initials upon review:_____							

COMMENTS: (Items needing repair or adjustment)

Date:	**Issue:**
Resolved Date:	**Resolved By:**
COMMENTS	

CAUTION: If the equipment is found to be in need of repair or in any way unsafe, or contributes to an unsafe condition, the matter shall be reported immediately to the designated authority and the equipment shall not be operated until it has been restored to safe condition. Do not make repairs or adjustments unless specifically authorized to do so.

- Inspect tire condition:
    - Pneumatic(air filled) wheels should have pressure and now have cracks through the rubber.
    - Solid wheels should not have large cracks or gouges in them.

- Check for grease and debris in the operator compartment – this can contribute to slipping off the equipment, and cause a serious injury.

- Hood & panel latches – Does the hood and any removable side panels secure in place to no avoid opening or falling off.

- Steering should function smoothly – while testing this, ensure the steering wheel solidly reacts to movements. This should always be monitored during operation.

- Check the functioning of horn and lights – this test is as simple as ensuring the lights aren't burnt out, and the horn operates.

- Back-up alarm (if equipped) should be checked – A backup alarm is a helpful piece of safety equipment. If equipped it must be operational, and not covered in any sound dampening material.

Week Ending: _____

The equipment operator must make this check daily at the start of the shift.

Check the appropriate box if the item is OK. If there is a problem with the item, leave the space blank and fill out the COMMENTS section below.

Visual Checks	Sun	Mon	Tues	Wed	Thur	Fri	Sat
EXCESS DIRT AND DEBRIS							
DAMAGE (Bent, dented or broken parts, paint transfer)							
LEAKS (Drive unit, brakes, hydraulics)							
TIRES & WHEELS (Drive wheels, load wheels, casters)							
FORKS (In place, properly secured, locking pins)							
CHAINS, CABLES, HOSES (In place)							
GUAGES (Operating)							
PROPANE BOTLE (relief valve, safety strap, fuel level, listen for leaks)							
ENGINE COMPARTMENT (oil, fan belt, battery, etc...)							
GUARDS (Overhead, load backrest, mast, etc.)							
SAFETY DEVICES (<u>Lights</u>, labels, seatbelt, harness, tether)							
MAST ASSEMBLY (no broken welds, no dents)							
Operational Checks	**REPORT ALL UNSAFE CONDITIONS**						
HORN (Sounds)							
STEERING (No binding, no excessive play)							
TRAVEL CONTROLS (All speed ranges, forward/reverse, etc.)							
HYDRAULIC CONTROLS (Raise & lover, tilt forward & back)							
BRAKES (Stop truck within required distance)							
PARKING BRAKE (Seat, hand, foot)							
POWER DISCONNECT (Cuts off all electric power)							
ATTACHMENTS (Function properly)							
EQUIPMENT WAS NOT USED ON THIS PARTICULAR DAY.							
OPERATOR'S INITIALS (PLEASE PRINT CLEARLY)							
Supervisor's Initials upon review:_____							

COMMENTS: (Items needing repair or adjustment)

Date:	Issue:
Resolved Date:	Resolved By:
COMMENTS	

CAUTION: If the equipment is found to be in need of repair or in any way unsafe, or contributes to an unsafe condition, the matter shall be reported immediately to the designated authority and the equipment shall not be operated until it has been restored to safe condition. Do not make repairs or adjustments unless specifically authorized to do so.

- Look out for any leaks, cracks, or visible defects in hydraulic hoses or tension in mast chains. – Checking for wet spots around hoses is how to identify hydraulic leaks, look visually around the hose connectors for cracks and bulges. Check along loop points for cracks, bulges, and frayed spots.

- Check fork condition including the top clip retaining pin and heel. – Forks should be able to be moved. Also inspect the tips of the forks, for curling or cracking.

- Check the load backrest extension and see if finger guards are attached. – Load backrest should be free from dents, deflections, or damage.

- Propane connectors for frayed tube or leaking connections. – propane connectors can become damaged over time, so visually inspect the cables and connectors for fraying on the cable and cracks or leaks on the connectors.

- Check if the **accelerator** or direction control pedal is working smoothly. – Inspect these as an operation test, by slowly moving the equipment.

- Tilt control: forward and back should be checked for smooth functioning. – Tilt the mast forward and back, quickly to verify operation is smooth and responsive.

Week Ending: _____

The equipment operator must make this check daily at the start of the shift.

Check the appropriate box if the item is OK. If there is a problem with the item, leave the space blank and fill out the COMMENTS section below.

Visual Checks	Sun	Mon	Tues	Wed	Thur	Fri	Sat
EXCESS DIRT AND DEBRIS							
DAMAGE (Bent, dented or broken parts, paint transfer)							
LEAKS (Drive unit, brakes, hydraulics)							
TIRES & WHEELS (Drive wheels, load wheels, casters)							
FORKS (In place, properly secured, locking pins)							
CHAINS, CABLES, HOSES (In place)							
GUAGES (Operating)							
PROPANE BOTLE (relief valve, safety strap, fuel level, listen for leaks)							
ENGINE COMPARTMENT (oil, fan belt, battery, etc…)							
GUARDS (Overhead, load backrest, mast, etc.)							
SAFETY DEVICES (<u>Lights</u>, labels, seatbelt, harness, tether)							
MAST ASSEMBLY (no broken welds, no dents)							
Operational Checks	REPORT ALL UNSAFE CONDITIONS						
HORN (Sounds)							
STEERING (No binding, no excessive play)							
TRAVEL CONTROLS (All speed ranges, forward/reverse, etc.)							
HYDRAULIC CONTROLS (Raise & lover, tilt forward & back)							
BRAKES (Stop truck within required distance)							
PARKING BRAKE (Seat, hand, foot)							
POWER DISCONNECT (Cuts off all electric power)							
ATTACHMENTS (Function properly)							
EQUIPMENT WAS NOT USED ON THIS PARTICULAR DAY.							
OPERATOR'S INITIALS (PLEASE PRINT CLEARLY)							
Supervisor's Initials upon review:_____							

COMMENTS: (Items needing repair or adjustment)

Date:	Issue:
Resolved Date:	**Resolved By:**
COMMENTS	

CAUTION: If the equipment is found to be in need of repair or in any way unsafe, or contributes to an unsafe condition, the matter shall be reported immediately to the designated authority and the equipment shall not be operated until it has been restored to safe condition. Do not make repairs or adjustments unless specifically authorized to do so.

- Inspect tire condition:
    - Pneumatic(air filled) wheels should have pressure and now have cracks through the rubber.
    - Solid wheels should not have large cracks or gouges in them.

- Check for grease and debris in the operator compartment – this can contribute to slipping off the equipment, and cause a serious injury.

- Hood & panel latches – Does the hood and any removable side panels secure in place to no avoid opening or falling off.

- Steering should function smoothly – while testing this, ensure the steering wheel solidly reacts to movements. This should always be monitored during operation.

- Check the functioning of horn and lights – this test is as simple as ensuring the lights aren't burnt out, and the horn operates.

- Back-up alarm (if equipped) should be checked – A backup alarm is a helpful piece of safety equipment. If equipped it must be operational, and not covered in any sound dampening material.

Week Ending: _____

The equipment operator must make this check daily at the start of the shift.

Check the appropriate box if the item is OK. If there is a problem with the item, leave the space blank and fill out the COMMENTS section below.

Visual Checks	Sun	Mon	Tues	Wed	Thur	Fri	Sat
EXCESS DIRT AND DEBRIS							
DAMAGE (Bent, dented or broken parts, paint transfer)							
LEAKS (Drive unit, brakes, hydraulics)							
TIRES & WHEELS (Drive wheels, load wheels, casters)							
FORKS (In place, properly secured, locking pins)							
CHAINS, CABLES, HOSES (In place)							
GUAGES (Operating)							
PROPANE BOTLE (relief valve, safety strap, fuel level, listen for leaks)							
ENGINE COMPARTMENT (oil, fan belt, battery, etc…)							
GUARDS (Overhead, load backrest, mast, etc.)							
SAFETY DEVICES (<u>Lights</u>, labels, seatbelt, harness, tether)							
MAST ASSEMBLY (no broken welds, no dents)							
Operational Checks	**REPORT ALL UNSAFE CONDITIONS**						
HORN (Sounds)							
STEERING (No binding, no excessive play)							
TRAVEL CONTROLS (All speed ranges, forward/reverse, etc.)							
HYDRAULIC CONTROLS (Raise & lover, tilt forward & back)							
BRAKES (Stop truck within required distance)							
PARKING BRAKE (Seat, hand, foot)							
POWER DISCONNECT (Cuts off all electric power)							
ATTACHMENTS (Function properly)							
EQUIPMENT WAS NOT USED ON THIS PARTICULAR DAY.							
OPERATOR'S INITIALS (PLEASE PRINT CLEARLY)							
Supervisor's Initials upon review:_____							

COMMENTS: (Items needing repair or adjustment)

Date:	Issue:
Resolved Date:	**Resolved By:**
COMMENTS	

CAUTION: If the equipment is found to be in need of repair or in any way unsafe, or contributes to an unsafe condition, the matter shall be reported immediately to the designated authority and the equipment shall not be operated until it has been restored to safe condition. Do not make repairs or adjustments unless specifically authorized to do so.

- Verify that all safety devices like the seat belt is in proper working condition – The seatbelt should be checked to ensure it locks on quick stops, and that it securely closes.

- Propane bottle restraints – The propane bottle should be secured in place with restraints, which must be locked in place.

- Propane level and connections – Check the level of the propane and the connection points, to ensure you have plenty of fuel for the safe operation and that it isn't leaking.

- Drive control - forward and reverse should be checked for smooth functioning.

- Hoist and lowering control should function smoothly – Check this by raising and lowering the mast, also at this point check the chain, to make sure it has adequate tension.

- Gauges: Functioning of Amp meter, engine oil pressure, Hour Meter, fuel level, temperature, and instrument monitors.

Week Ending: _____

The equipment operator must make this check daily at the start of the shift.

Check the appropriate box if the item is OK. If there is a problem with the item, leave the space blank and fill out the COMMENTS section below.

Visual Checks	Sun	Mon	Tues	Wed	Thur	Fri	Sat
EXCESS DIRT AND DEBRIS							
DAMAGE (Bent, dented or broken parts, paint transfer)							
LEAKS (Drive unit, brakes, hydraulics)							
TIRES & WHEELS (Drive wheels, load wheels, casters)							
FORKS (In place, properly secured, locking pins)							
CHAINS, CABLES, HOSES (In place)							
GUAGES (Operating)							
PROPANE BOTLE (relief valve, safety strap, fuel level, listen for leaks)							
ENGINE COMPARTMENT (oil, fan belt, battery, etc…)							
GUARDS (Overhead, load backrest, mast, etc.)							
SAFETY DEVICES (<u>Lights</u>, labels, seatbelt, harness, tether)							
MAST ASSEMBLY (no broken welds, no dents)							
Operational Checks	REPORT ALL UNSAFE CONDITIONS						
HORN (Sounds)							
STEERING (No binding, no excessive play)							
TRAVEL CONTROLS (All speed ranges, forward/reverse, etc.)							
HYDRAULIC CONTROLS (Raise & lover, tilt forward & back)							
BRAKES (Stop truck within required distance)							
PARKING BRAKE (Seat, hand, foot)							
POWER DISCONNECT (Cuts off all electric power)							
ATTACHMENTS (Function properly)							
EQUIPMENT WAS NOT USED ON THIS PARTICULAR DAY.							
OPERATOR'S INITIALS (PLEASE PRINT CLEARLY)							

Supervisor's Initials upon review:_____

COMMENTS: (Items needing repair or adjustment)

Date:	Issue:
Resolved Date:	**Resolved By:**
COMMENTS	

CAUTION: If the equipment is found to be in need of repair or in any way unsafe, or contributes to an unsafe condition, the matter shall be reported immediately to the designated authority and the equipment shall not be operated until it has been restored to safe condition. Do not make repairs or adjustments unless specifically authorized to do so.

- Inspect tire condition:
  - Pneumatic(air filled) wheels should have pressure and now have cracks through the rubber.
  - Solid wheels should not have large cracks or gouges in them.

- Check for grease and debris in the operator compartment – this can contribute to slipping off the equipment, and cause a serious injury.

- Hood & panel latches – Does the hood and any removable side panels secure in place to no avoid opening or falling off.

- Steering should function smoothly – while testing this, ensure the steering wheel solidly reacts to movements. This should always be monitored during operation.

- Check the functioning of horn and lights – this test is as simple as ensuring the lights aren't burnt out, and the horn operates.

- Back-up alarm (if equipped) should be checked – A backup alarm is a helpful piece of safety equipment. If equipped it must be operational, and not covered in any sound dampening material.

Week Ending: _____

The equipment operator must make this check daily at the start of the shift.

Check the appropriate box if the item is OK. If there is a problem with the item, leave the space blank and fill out the COMMENTS section below.

Visual Checks	Sun	Mon	Tues	Wed	Thur	Fri	Sat
EXCESS DIRT AND DEBRIS							
DAMAGE (Bent, dented or broken parts, paint transfer)							
LEAKS (Drive unit, brakes, hydraulics)							
TIRES & WHEELS (Drive wheels, load wheels, casters)							
FORKS (In place, properly secured, locking pins)							
CHAINS, CABLES, HOSES (In place)							
GUAGES (Operating)							
PROPANE BOTLE (relief valve, safety strap, fuel level, listen for leaks)							
ENGINE COMPARTMENT (oil, fan belt, battery, etc…)							
GUARDS (Overhead, load backrest, mast, etc.)							
SAFETY DEVICES (<u>Lights</u>, labels, seatbelt, harness, tether)							
MAST ASSEMBLY (no broken welds, no dents)							
Operational Checks	**REPORT ALL UNSAFE CONDITIONS**						
HORN (Sounds)							
STEERING (No binding, no excessive play)							
TRAVEL CONTROLS (All speed ranges, forward/reverse, etc.)							
HYDRAULIC CONTROLS (Raise & lover, tilt forward & back)							
BRAKES (Stop truck within required distance)							
PARKING BRAKE (Seat, hand, foot)							
POWER DISCONNECT (Cuts off all electric power)							
ATTACHMENTS (Function properly)							
EQUIPMENT WAS NOT USED ON THIS PARTICULAR DAY.							
OPERATOR'S INITIALS (PLEASE PRINT CLEARLY)							

Supervisor's Initials upon review:_____

COMMENTS: (Items needing repair or adjustment)

Date:	Issue:
Resolved Date:	**Resolved By:**
COMMENTS	

CAUTION: If the equipment is found to be in need of repair or in any way unsafe, or contributes to an unsafe condition, the matter shall be reported immediately to the designated authority and the equipment shall not be operated until it has been restored to safe condition. Do not make repairs or adjustments unless specifically authorized to do so.

- Look out for any leaks, cracks, or visible defects in hydraulic hoses or tension in mast chains. – Checking for wet spots around hoses is how to identify hydraulic leaks, look visually around the hose connectors for cracks and bulges. Check along loop points for cracks, bulges, and frayed spots.

- Check fork condition including the top clip retaining pin and heel. – Forks should be able to be moved. Also inspect the tips of the forks, for curling or cracking.

- Check the load backrest extension and see if finger guards are attached. – Load backrest should be free from dents, deflections, or damage.

- Propane connectors for frayed tube or leaking connections. – propane connectors can become damaged over time, so visually inspect the cables and connectors for fraying on the cable and cracks or leaks on the connectors.

- Check if the **accelerator** or direction control pedal is working smoothly. – Inspect these as an operation test, by slowly moving the equipment.

- Tilt control: forward and back should be checked for smooth functioning. – Tilt the mast forward and back, quickly to verify operation is smooth and responsive.

Week Ending: _____

The equipment operator must make this check daily at the start of the shift.

Check the appropriate box if the item is OK. If there is a problem with the item, leave the space blank and fill out the COMMENTS section below.

Visual Checks	Sun	Mon	Tues	Wed	Thur	Fri	Sat
EXCESS DIRT AND DEBRIS							
DAMAGE (Bent, dented or broken parts, paint transfer)							
LEAKS (Drive unit, brakes, hydraulics)							
TIRES & WHEELS (Drive wheels, load wheels, casters)							
FORKS (In place, properly secured, locking pins)							
CHAINS, CABLES, HOSES (In place)							
GUAGES (Operating)							
PROPANE BOTLE (relief valve, safety strap, fuel level, listen for leaks)							
ENGINE COMPARTMENT (oil, fan belt, battery, etc…)							
GUARDS (Overhead, load backrest, mast, etc.)							
SAFETY DEVICES (<u>Lights</u>, labels, seatbelt, harness, tether)							
MAST ASSEMBLY (no broken welds, no dents)							
Operational Checks	REPORT ALL UNSAFE CONDITIONS						
HORN (Sounds)							
STEERING (No binding, no excessive play)							
TRAVEL CONTROLS (All speed ranges, forward/reverse, etc.)							
HYDRAULIC CONTROLS (Raise & lover, tilt forward & back)							
BRAKES (Stop truck within required distance)							
PARKING BRAKE (Seat, hand, foot)							
POWER DISCONNECT (Cuts off all electric power)							
ATTACHMENTS (Function properly)							
EQUIPMENT WAS NOT USED ON THIS PARTICULAR DAY.							
OPERATOR'S INITIALS (PLEASE PRINT CLEARLY)							
Supervisor's Initials upon review:_____							

COMMENTS: (Items needing repair or adjustment)

Date:	Issue:
Resolved Date:	**Resolved By:**
COMMENTS	

CAUTION: If the equipment is found to be in need of repair or in any way unsafe, or contributes to an unsafe condition, the matter shall be reported immediately to the designated authority and the equipment shall not be operated until it has been restored to safe condition. Do not make repairs or adjustments unless specifically authorized to do so.

- Inspect tire condition:
  - Pneumatic(air filled) wheels should have pressure and now have cracks through the rubber.
  - Solid wheels should not have large cracks or gouges in them.

- Check for grease and debris in the operator compartment – this can contribute to slipping off the equipment, and cause a serious injury.

- Hood & panel latches – Does the hood and any removable side panels secure in place to no avoid opening or falling off.

- Steering should function smoothly – while testing this, ensure the steering wheel solidly reacts to movements. This should always be monitored during operation.

- Check the functioning of horn and lights – this test is as simple as ensuring the lights aren't burnt out, and the horn operates.

- Back-up alarm (if equipped) should be checked – A backup alarm is a helpful piece of safety equipment. If equipped it must be operational, and not covered in any sound dampening material.

Week Ending: _____

The equipment operator must make this check daily at the start of the shift.

Check the appropriate box if the item is OK. If there is a problem with the item, leave the space blank and fill out the COMMENTS section below.

Visual Checks	Sun	Mon	Tues	Wed	Thur	Fri	Sat
EXCESS DIRT AND DEBRIS							
DAMAGE (Bent, dented or broken parts, paint transfer)							
LEAKS (Drive unit, brakes, hydraulics)							
TIRES & WHEELS (Drive wheels, load wheels, casters)							
FORKS (In place, properly secured, locking pins)							
CHAINS, CABLES, HOSES (In place)							
GUAGES (Operating)							
PROPANE BOTLE (relief valve, safety strap, fuel level, listen for leaks)							
ENGINE COMPARTMENT (oil, fan belt, battery, etc…)							
GUARDS (Overhead, load backrest, mast, etc.)							
SAFETY DEVICES (<u>Lights</u>, labels, seatbelt, harness, tether)							
MAST ASSEMBLY (no broken welds, no dents)							
Operational Checks	**REPORT ALL UNSAFE CONDITIONS**						
HORN (Sounds)							
STEERING (No binding, no excessive play)							
TRAVEL CONTROLS (All speed ranges, forward/reverse, etc.)							
HYDRAULIC CONTROLS (Raise & lover, tilt forward & back)							
BRAKES (Stop truck within required distance)							
PARKING BRAKE (Seat, hand, foot)							
POWER DISCONNECT (Cuts off all electric power)							
ATTACHMENTS (Function properly)							
EQUIPMENT WAS NOT USED ON THIS PARTICULAR DAY.							
OPERATOR'S INITIALS (PLEASE PRINT CLEARLY)							

Supervisor's Initials upon review:_____

COMMENTS: (Items needing repair or adjustment)

Date:	Issue:
Resolved Date:	**Resolved By:**
COMMENTS	

CAUTION: If the equipment is found to be in need of repair or in any way unsafe, or contributes to an unsafe condition, the matter shall be reported immediately to the designated authority and the equipment shall not be operated until it has been restored to safe condition. Do not make repairs or adjustments unless specifically authorized to do so.

- Verify that all safety devices like the seat belt is in proper working condition – The seatbelt should be checked to ensure it locks on quick stops, and that it securely closes.

- Propane bottle restraints – The propane bottle should be secured in place with restraints, which must be locked in place.

- Propane level and connections – Check the level of the propane and the connection points, to ensure you have plenty of fuel for the safe operation and that it isn't leaking.

- Drive control - forward and reverse should be checked for smooth functioning.

- Hoist and lowering control should function smoothly – Check this by raising and lowering the mast, also at this point check the chain, to make sure it has adequate tension.

- Gauges: Functioning of Amp meter, engine oil pressure, Hour Meter, fuel level, temperature, and instrument monitors.

Week Ending: _____

The equipment operator must make this check daily at the start of the shift.

Check the appropriate box if the item is OK. If there is a problem with the item, leave the space blank and fill out the COMMENTS section below.

Visual Checks	Sun	Mon	Tues	Wed	Thur	Fri	Sat
EXCESS DIRT AND DEBRIS							
DAMAGE (Bent, dented or broken parts, paint transfer)							
LEAKS (Drive unit, brakes, hydraulics)							
TIRES & WHEELS (Drive wheels, load wheels, casters)							
FORKS (In place, properly secured, locking pins)							
CHAINS, CABLES, HOSES (In place)							
GUAGES (Operating)							
PROPANE BOTLE (relief valve, safety strap, fuel level, listen for leaks)							
ENGINE COMPARTMENT (oil, fan belt, battery, etc...)							
GUARDS (Overhead, load backrest, mast, etc.)							
SAFETY DEVICES (<u>Lights</u>, labels, seatbelt, harness, tether)							
MAST ASSEMBLY (no broken welds, no dents)							
Operational Checks	REPORT ALL UNSAFE CONDITIONS						
HORN (Sounds)							
STEERING (No binding, no excessive play)							
TRAVEL CONTROLS (All speed ranges, forward/reverse, etc.)							
HYDRAULIC CONTROLS (Raise & lover, tilt forward & back)							
BRAKES (Stop truck within required distance)							
PARKING BRAKE (Seat, hand, foot)							
POWER DISCONNECT (Cuts off all electric power)							
ATTACHMENTS (Function properly)							
EQUIPMENT WAS NOT USED ON THIS PARTICULAR DAY.							
OPERATOR'S INITIALS (PLEASE PRINT CLEARLY)							

Supervisor's Initials upon review:_____

COMMENTS: (Items needing repair or adjustment)

Date:	Issue:
Resolved Date:	**Resolved By:**
COMMENTS	

CAUTION: If the equipment is found to be in need of repair or in any way unsafe, or contributes to an unsafe condition, the matter shall be reported immediately to the designated authority and the equipment shall not be operated until it has been restored to safe condition. Do not make repairs or adjustments unless specifically authorized to do so.

- Inspect tire condition:
  - Pneumatic(air filled) wheels should have pressure and now have cracks through the rubber.
  - Solid wheels should not have large cracks or gouges in them.

- Check for grease and debris in the operator compartment – this can contribute to slipping off the equipment, and cause a serious injury.

- Hood & panel latches – Does the hood and any removable side panels secure in place to no avoid opening or falling off.

- Steering should function smoothly – while testing this, ensure the steering wheel solidly reacts to movements. This should always be monitored during operation.

- Check the functioning of horn and lights – this test is as simple as ensuring the lights aren't burnt out, and the horn operates.

- Back-up alarm (if equipped) should be checked – A backup alarm is a helpful piece of safety equipment. If equipped it must be operational, and not covered in any sound dampening material.

Week Ending: _____

The equipment operator must make this check daily at the start of the shift.

Check the appropriate box if the item is OK. If there is a problem with the item, leave the space blank and fill out the COMMENTS section below.

Visual Checks	Sun	Mon	Tues	Wed	Thur	Fri	Sat
EXCESS DIRT AND DEBRIS							
DAMAGE (Bent, dented or broken parts, paint transfer)							
LEAKS (Drive unit, brakes, hydraulics)							
TIRES & WHEELS (Drive wheels, load wheels, casters)							
FORKS (In place, properly secured, locking pins)							
CHAINS, CABLES, HOSES (In place)							
GUAGES (Operating)							
PROPANE BOTLE (relief valve, safety strap, fuel level, listen for leaks)							
ENGINE COMPARTMENT (oil, fan belt, battery, etc...)							
GUARDS (Overhead, load backrest, mast, etc.)							
SAFETY DEVICES (<u>Lights</u>, labels, seatbelt, harness, tether)							
MAST ASSEMBLY (no broken welds, no dents)							
Operational Checks	**REPORT ALL UNSAFE CONDITIONS**						
HORN (Sounds)							
STEERING (No binding, no excessive play)							
TRAVEL CONTROLS (All speed ranges, forward/reverse, etc.)							
HYDRAULIC CONTROLS (Raise & lover, tilt forward & back)							
BRAKES (Stop truck within required distance)							
PARKING BRAKE (Seat, hand, foot)							
POWER DISCONNECT (Cuts off all electric power)							
ATTACHMENTS (Function properly)							
EQUIPMENT WAS NOT USED ON THIS PARTICULAR DAY.							
OPERATOR'S INITIALS (PLEASE PRINT CLEARLY)							
Supervisor's Initials upon review:_____							

COMMENTS: (Items needing repair or adjustment)

Date:	Issue:
Resolved Date:	**Resolved By:**
COMMENTS	

CAUTION: If the equipment is found to be in need of repair or in any way unsafe, or contributes to an unsafe condition, the matter shall be reported immediately to the designated authority and the equipment shall not be operated until it has been restored to safe condition. Do not make repairs or adjustments unless specifically authorized to do so.

- Look out for any leaks, cracks, or visible defects in hydraulic hoses or tension in mast chains. – Checking for wet spots around hoses is how to identify hydraulic leaks, look visually around the hose connectors for cracks and bulges. Check along loop points for cracks, bulges, and frayed spots.

- Check fork condition including the top clip retaining pin and heel. – Forks should be able to be moved. Also inspect the tips of the forks, for curling or cracking.

- Check the load backrest extension and see if finger guards are attached. – Load backrest should be free from dents, deflections, or damage.

- Propane connectors for frayed tube or leaking connections. – propane connectors can become damaged over time, so visually inspect the cables and connectors for fraying on the cable and cracks or leaks on the connectors.

- Check if the **accelerator** or direction control pedal is working smoothly. – Inspect these as an operation test, by slowly moving the equipment.

- Tilt control: forward and back should be checked for smooth functioning. – Tilt the mast forward and back, quickly to verify operation is smooth and responsive.

Week Ending: _____

The equipment operator must make this check daily at the start of the shift.

Check the appropriate box if the item is OK. If there is a problem with the item, leave the space blank and fill out the COMMENTS section below.

Visual Checks	Sun	Mon	Tues	Wed	Thur	Fri	Sat
EXCESS DIRT AND DEBRIS							
DAMAGE (Bent, dented or broken parts, paint transfer)							
LEAKS (Drive unit, brakes, hydraulics)							
TIRES & WHEELS (Drive wheels, load wheels, casters)							
FORKS (In place, properly secured, locking pins)							
CHAINS, CABLES, HOSES (In place)							
GUAGES (Operating)							
PROPANE BOTLE (relief valve, safety strap, fuel level, listen for leaks)							
ENGINE COMPARTMENT (oil, fan belt, battery, etc…)							
GUARDS (Overhead, load backrest, mast, etc.)							
SAFETY DEVICES (<u>Lights</u>, labels, seatbelt, harness, tether)							
MAST ASSEMBLY (no broken welds, no dents)							
Operational Checks	REPORT ALL UNSAFE CONDITIONS						
HORN (Sounds)							
STEERING (No binding, no excessive play)							
TRAVEL CONTROLS (All speed ranges, forward/reverse, etc.)							
HYDRAULIC CONTROLS (Raise & lover, tilt forward & back)							
BRAKES (Stop truck within required distance)							
PARKING BRAKE (Seat, hand, foot)							
POWER DISCONNECT (Cuts off all electric power)							
ATTACHMENTS (Function properly)							
EQUIPMENT WAS NOT USED ON THIS PARTICULAR DAY.							
OPERATOR'S INITIALS (PLEASE PRINT CLEARLY)							

Supervisor's Initials upon review:_____

COMMENTS: (Items needing repair or adjustment)

Date:	Issue:
Resolved Date:	**Resolved By:**
COMMENTS	

CAUTION: If the equipment is found to be in need of repair or in any way unsafe, or contributes to an unsafe condition, the matter shall be reported immediately to the designated authority and the equipment shall not be operated until it has been restored to safe condition. Do not make repairs or adjustments unless specifically authorized to do so.

- Inspect tire condition:
  - Pneumatic(air filled) wheels should have pressure and now have cracks through the rubber.
  - Solid wheels should not have large cracks or gouges in them.

- Check for grease and debris in the operator compartment – this can contribute to slipping off the equipment, and cause a serious injury.

- Hood & panel latches – Does the hood and any removable side panels secure in place to no avoid opening or falling off.

- Steering should function smoothly – while testing this, ensure the steering wheel solidly reacts to movements. This should always be monitored during operation.

- Check the functioning of horn and lights – this test is as simple as ensuring the lights aren't burnt out, and the horn operates.

- Back-up alarm (if equipped) should be checked – A backup alarm is a helpful piece of safety equipment. If equipped it must be operational, and not covered in any sound dampening material.

Week Ending: _____

The equipment operator must make this check daily at the start of the shift.

Check the appropriate box if the item is OK. If there is a problem with the item, leave the space blank and fill out the COMMENTS section below.

Visual Checks	Sun	Mon	Tues	Wed	Thur	Fri	Sat
EXCESS DIRT AND DEBRIS							
DAMAGE (Bent, dented or broken parts, paint transfer)							
LEAKS (Drive unit, brakes, hydraulics)							
TIRES & WHEELS (Drive wheels, load wheels, casters)							
FORKS (In place, properly secured, locking pins)							
CHAINS, CABLES, HOSES (In place)							
GUAGES (Operating)							
PROPANE BOTLE (relief valve, safety strap, fuel level, listen for leaks)							
ENGINE COMPARTMENT (oil, fan belt, battery, etc...)							
GUARDS (Overhead, load backrest, mast, etc.)							
SAFETY DEVICES (<u>Lights</u>, labels, seatbelt, harness, tether)							
MAST ASSEMBLY (no broken welds, no dents)							
Operational Checks	REPORT ALL UNSAFE CONDITIONS						
HORN (Sounds)							
STEERING (No binding, no excessive play)							
TRAVEL CONTROLS (All speed ranges, forward/reverse, etc.)							
HYDRAULIC CONTROLS (Raise & lover, tilt forward & back)							
BRAKES (Stop truck within required distance)							
PARKING BRAKE (Seat, hand, foot)							
POWER DISCONNECT (Cuts off all electric power)							
ATTACHMENTS (Function properly)							
EQUIPMENT WAS NOT USED ON THIS PARTICULAR DAY.							
OPERATOR'S INITIALS (PLEASE PRINT CLEARLY)							
Supervisor's Initials upon review:_____							

COMMENTS: (Items needing repair or adjustment)

Date:	Issue:
Resolved Date:	**Resolved By:**
COMMENTS	

CAUTION: If the equipment is found to be in need of repair or in any way unsafe, or contributes to an unsafe condition, the matter shall be reported immediately to the designated authority and the equipment shall not be operated until it has been restored to safe condition. Do not make repairs or adjustments unless specifically authorized to do so.

- Verify that all safety devices like the seat belt is in proper working condition – The seatbelt should be checked to ensure it locks on quick stops, and that it securely closes.

- Propane bottle restraints – The propane bottle should be secured in place with restraints, which must be locked in place.

- Propane level and connections – Check the level of the propane and the connection points, to ensure you have plenty of fuel for the safe operation and that it isn't leaking.

- Drive control - forward and reverse should be checked for smooth functioning.

- Hoist and lowering control should function smoothly – Check this by raising and lowering the mast, also at this point check the chain, to make sure it has adequate tension.

- Gauges: Functioning of Amp meter, engine oil pressure, Hour Meter, fuel level, temperature, and instrument monitors.

Week Ending: _____

The equipment operator must make this check daily at the start of the shift.

Check the appropriate box if the item is OK. If there is a problem with the item, leave the space blank and fill out the COMMENTS section below.

Visual Checks	Sun	Mon	Tues	Wed	Thur	Fri	Sat
EXCESS DIRT AND DEBRIS							
DAMAGE (Bent, dented or broken parts, paint transfer)							
LEAKS (Drive unit, brakes, hydraulics)							
TIRES & WHEELS (Drive wheels, load wheels, casters)							
FORKS (In place, properly secured, locking pins)							
CHAINS, CABLES, HOSES (In place)							
GUAGES (Operating)							
PROPANE BOTLE (relief valve, safety strap, fuel level, listen for leaks)							
ENGINE COMPARTMENT (oil, fan belt, battery, etc…)							
GUARDS (Overhead, load backrest, mast, etc.)							
SAFETY DEVICES (<u>Lights</u>, labels, seatbelt, harness, tether)							
MAST ASSEMBLY (no broken welds, no dents)							
Operational Checks	REPORT ALL UNSAFE CONDITIONS						
HORN (Sounds)							
STEERING (No binding, no excessive play)							
TRAVEL CONTROLS (All speed ranges, forward/reverse, etc.)							
HYDRAULIC CONTROLS (Raise & lover, tilt forward & back)							
BRAKES (Stop truck within required distance)							
PARKING BRAKE (Seat, hand, foot)							
POWER DISCONNECT (Cuts off all electric power)							
ATTACHMENTS (Function properly)							
EQUIPMENT WAS NOT USED ON THIS PARTICULAR DAY.							
OPERATOR'S INITIALS (PLEASE PRINT CLEARLY)							
Supervisor's Initials upon review:_____							

COMMENTS: (Items needing repair or adjustment)

Date:	Issue:
Resolved Date:	**Resolved By:**
COMMENTS	

CAUTION: If the equipment is found to be in need of repair or in any way unsafe, or contributes to an unsafe condition, the matter shall be reported immediately to the designated authority and the equipment shall not be operated until it has been restored to safe condition. Do not make repairs or adjustments unless specifically authorized to do so.

- Inspect tire condition:
    - Pneumatic(air filled) wheels should have pressure and now have cracks through the rubber.
    - Solid wheels should not have large cracks or gouges in them.

- Check for grease and debris in the operator compartment – this can contribute to slipping off the equipment, and cause a serious injury.

- Hood & panel latches – Does the hood and any removable side panels secure in place to no avoid opening or falling off.

- Steering should function smoothly – while testing this, ensure the steering wheel solidly reacts to movements. This should always be monitored during operation.

- Check the functioning of horn and lights – this test is as simple as ensuring the lights aren't burnt out, and the horn operates.

- Back-up alarm (if equipped) should be checked – A backup alarm is a helpful piece of safety equipment. If equipped it must be operational, and not covered in any sound dampening material.

Week Ending: _____

The equipment operator must make this check daily at the start of the shift.

Check the appropriate box if the item is OK. If there is a problem with the item, leave the space blank and fill out the COMMENTS section below.

Visual Checks	Sun	Mon	Tues	Wed	Thur	Fri	Sat
EXCESS DIRT AND DEBRIS							
DAMAGE (Bent, dented or broken parts, paint transfer)							
LEAKS (Drive unit, brakes, hydraulics)							
TIRES & WHEELS (Drive wheels, load wheels, casters)							
FORKS (In place, properly secured, locking pins)							
CHAINS, CABLES, HOSES (In place)							
GUAGES (Operating)							
PROPANE BOTLE (relief valve, safety strap, fuel level, listen for leaks)							
ENGINE COMPARTMENT (oil, fan belt, battery, etc…)							
GUARDS (Overhead, load backrest, mast, etc.)							
SAFETY DEVICES (<u>Lights</u>, labels, seatbelt, harness, tether)							
MAST ASSEMBLY (no broken welds, no dents)							
Operational Checks	**REPORT ALL UNSAFE CONDITIONS**						
HORN (Sounds)							
STEERING (No binding, no excessive play)							
TRAVEL CONTROLS (All speed ranges, forward/reverse, etc.)							
HYDRAULIC CONTROLS (Raise & lover, tilt forward & back)							
BRAKES (Stop truck within required distance)							
PARKING BRAKE (Seat, hand, foot)							
POWER DISCONNECT (Cuts off all electric power)							
ATTACHMENTS (Function properly)							
EQUIPMENT WAS NOT USED ON THIS PARTICULAR DAY.							
OPERATOR'S INITIALS (PLEASE PRINT CLEARLY)							
Supervisor's Initials upon review:_____							

COMMENTS: (Items needing repair or adjustment)

Date:	Issue:
Resolved Date:	**Resolved By:**
COMMENTS	

CAUTION: If the equipment is found to be in need of repair or in any way unsafe, or contributes to an unsafe condition, the matter shall be reported immediately to the designated authority and the equipment shall not be operated until it has been restored to safe condition. Do not make repairs or adjustments unless specifically authorized to do so.